I Am the Utterance of My Name

I Am the Utterance of My Name

◆

Black Victorian Feminist Discourse and Intellectual Enterprise at the Columbian Exposition, 1893

Temple Tsenes-Hills, Ph.D.

iUniverse, Inc.
New York Lincoln Shanghai

I Am the Utterance of My Name
Black Victorian Feminist Discourse and Intellectual Enterprise at the Columbian Exposition, 1893

iUniverse books may be ordered through booksellers or by contacting:

iUniverse
2021 Pine Lake Road, Suite 100
Lincoln, NE 68512
www.iuniverse.com
1-800-Authors (1-800-288-4677)

ISBN-13: 978-0-595-40687-6 (pbk)
ISBN-13: 978-0-595-85051-8 (ebk)
ISBN-10: 0-595-40687-4 (pbk)
ISBN-10: 0-595-85051-0 (ebk)

Printed in the United States of America

For my mother
Dorothy Elizabeth Tsenes
Strength, Beauty, Wisdom, Love

For my husband
Peter William Hills
Everything, Always

For my children
Rory, Sage, Never, and Deme
Light, Laughter, Joy, Angel

Whatever she planted grew as if by magic...A garden so brilliant with colors, so original in its design, so magnificent with life and creativity...she is radiant, almost to the point of being invisible—except as Creator; hand and eye. She is involved in work her soul must have. Ordering the universe in the image of her personal conception of beauty...a legacy of respect she leaves to me, for all that illuminates and cherishes life. She has handed down respect for the possibilities—and the will to grasp them...This ability to hold on, even in very simple ways, is work black women have done for a very long time...Guided by my heritage of a love of beauty and a respect for strength—in search of my mother's garden, I found my own.

—Alice Walker, *In Search of Our Mothers' Gardens*

Contents

1

SHARPENING MY OYSTER KNIFE, AN INTRODUCTION

I am not tragically colored. There is no great sorrow damned up in my soul, nor lurking behind my eyes. No, I do not weep at the world—I am too busy sharpening my oyster knife.

—Zora Neale Hurston, *How it Feels to be Colored Me*

"I Am the Utterance of My Name: Black Victorian Feminist Discourse and Intellectual Enterprise at the Columbian Exposition, 1893" is not so much about the activities of the White City and Midway Plaisance of the Columbian Exposition.[1] It is about utilizing the Exposition, particularly the palpable presence of African American women at the World's Congress of Representative Women, as a historical illustration of a distinct Black feminist discourse and intellectual enterprise[2]. In 1892 the National Commission that oversaw the planning and implementation of the Exposition, elected to hold a formal assembly, a World's Congress. The purpose of this congress was to discuss universally acknowledged social, political and cultural issues of the day. Several congresses were formed to discuss such topics as language, literature, religion, science, art, education, industry, poverty and domestic life. The Board of Lady Managers, the auxiliary arm of the National Commission, formed a Women's World Congress Committee whose purpose was to oversee the planning and implementation of a World's Congress of Representative Women.

The primary focus of this women's congress was to share with the world the fruits of nineteenth-century women's intellectual discourse and enterprise, women's contributions to the evolution of civilization, and women's commitment to the procurement of empowering changes for women around the world. The congress featured more than six hundred speakers from twenty countries, representing one hundred and twenty-six national and international women's organizations. Six African American women were invited to participate in the World's Congress of Representative Women and Ida B. Wells made her mark through her creation and publication of *The Reason Why the Colored American is Not at the Columbian Exposition* and through her post at the Haitian Building where she distributed ten thousand copies of her pamphlet during the last three months of the Exposition. Hazel V. Carby suggests that the participation of African American women at the congress was less recognition, by the National Commission and Board of Lady Managers, of their right to be there than it was a part of "…a discourse of exoticism that pervaded the fair. Black Americans were included in a highly selective manner…[it was an] attempt to scientifically legitimate racist assumptions."[3] The Board of Lady Managers may have attempted to present these women as archetypes of accepted nineteenth-century stereotypes of African Americans but they, and the world, got much more than they bargained for! These seven women were not representative denizens of some exotic other world. These women engaged in a tangible act of individual and collective identity re-formation; an act of *willed creation*: the reconstruction and elevation of Black womanhood.

The heart of this dissertation revolves around the addresses of Hallie Quinn Brown, Anna Julia Cooper, Fanny Jackson Coppin, Sarah Jane Early, Frances Ellen Watkins Harper, and Fannie Barrier Williams, at the World's Congress of Representative Women and the creation, publication, and distribution of Ida B. Wells' protest pamphlet *The Reason Why the Colored American is Not at the Columbian Exposition*. Several factors critically informed the content of the addresses and the creation of Wells' pamphlet: a quest for the acquisition of personal and communal power through a doctrine based in the concept of the elevation of Black womanhood; an ideology of racial solidarity; a historical foundation of a Black feminist ethos; and a unique Victorian sensibility. These seven women articulated a standpoint that emanated from a distinct consciousness, culture, and experience; in so doing they spoke profoundly about what it meant to be Black and woman in turn-of-the-century America. Moreover, these seven women were emissaries from a Black Victorian Feminist movement.

The theoretical foundation of my research is grounded in a particular set of assumptions. First, Black women's history is a singular phenomenon. Second, this phenomenon has definite characteristics. Third, a particular method of analysis for this phenomenon is essential in order to discover and examine the historical implications of Black women's involvement at the Exposition. African American women have historically been the inhabitants of a distinct culture, consciousness, and community. Their experiences have always been, and still are, heterogeneous. Nevertheless, nineteenth century Black women shared the common experience of racism, sexism, and classism—a *triad of oppression*. This triad of oppression, an essential component in African American woman's history, suggests four core themes: the legacy of struggle, the search for voice, the interdependence of thought and action, and the importance of empowerment in everyday life.[4]

The first core theme is *the legacy of struggle*, or the importance of thinking inclusively about how the triad of oppression shaped Black women's lives. This viewpoint necessitates examination of the *links between* the identity variables of race, gender, and class as opposed to defining and presenting them as unrelated, ahistorical, social constructs. "This legacy has fostered a heightened consciousness among Black women intellectuals about the importance of thinking inclusively about how race, class, and gender shape Black women's lives."[5] The socio-cultural construction of the idealized 'slave' woman, for example, was a direct result of American society's attempt to reconcile and rationalize enslaved women's existence with prevalent constructions of idealized gender and racial roles in conjunction with religious attitudes. Yet, while white America mythologized the elite white woman as the model of femininity for the world to emulate, Black women relied on their own standards of true womanhood. For enslaved women idealized notions of female passivity and helplessness were fallacious.

The *search for voice*, or the manner in which Black women negotiated and/or refuted the damaging and controlling images/stereotypes of themselves and also created and promoted a self-defined and self-valuated image, is the second core theme. "In order to exploit Black women, dominant groups have developed controlling images or stereotypes claiming that Black women are inferior. Because they justify Black women's oppression...interrelated controlling images of Black women—the mammy...and the jezebel—reflect the dominant group's interest in maintaining Black women's subordination. [These images] are so negative that they require resistance..."[6] Self-definition involves challenging negative and damaging stereotypes of Black womanhood and speaks to the power dynamics involved in the *act* of identity re-formation (personal and communal). Self-valuation involves the actual *content* of these self-definitions (i.e. the deliberate construction of Black womanhood). "Individual women [who chose] to be self-defined and self-evaluating [were], in fact, activists...Moreover, if these black women used all their resources to not only be self-defined and self-evaluated, but to also encourage their sisters in bondage and freedom to do the same, then black women's everyday behavior itself is a form of activism."[7]

The *interdependence of thought and action*, or the need to relate Black women's experience to intellectual inquiry, is the third core theme. To focus on Black woman's culture and intellectual production illustrates the complex nature of activism. Brenda E. Stevenson explores and discusses some of the positive images that enslaved women created of, and for, themselves.[8] Through the 'vehicle' of the autobiographical story, some enslaved women were able to construct what, for them, was an operative legitimate identity, a counterimage to the larger society's construction of demeaning stereotypes of Black womanhood. There are numerous stories, for example, about the rape and physical abuse that enslaved women endured. Most of these women could not fight back, except perhaps in the testimony of their painful stories, which vindicated their assertion of sexual morality. Those women who did fight back emerged in the lore and mythology of enslaved women—both as models for Black women's conduct and as symbols of resistance that engendered a sense of pride. "It is this interrelationship between thought and action that allows Black women to see the connections among concrete experiences with oppression, to develop a self-defined voice concerning those experiences, and to enact the resistance that can follow."[9]

Finally, the fourth core theme is the *importance of empowerment in everyday life*, or the desire of Black women to utilize their individual and collective voices to create a 'space' within which they could participate in the ownership and accountability for their lives and the world in which they lived. "Black feminist thought sees Black women's oppression and their resistance to oppression as inextricably linked. Thus, oppression responds to human action."[10] One such response to oppression was Black women's development of a 'culture of dissemblance'—the erection of a veil of secrecy to shield the truth of the inner lives of Black women from the larger (white) society.[11] The culture of dissemblance was an integral part of the enslaved woman's community and, by necessity, this method of self-imposed invisibility extended into the nineteenth century Black woman's community and culture, providing yet another avenue by which Black women could create, sustain and promulgate positive images among themselves, 'safe' from the damaging elements of the larger society.

By the late nineteenth century the triad of oppression, buttressed by segregation and disenfranchisement, threatened the advancement of the post-Slaveocratic Black community. In the face of pervasive and hostile conditions it was clear that African Americans would have to devise and implement their own strategies of social, political and cultural advancement. Nineteenth century Black intellectuals and community activists sought to realize the goals and aspirations of the larger Black community through the development of a concept of racial solidarity defined by a distinct cultural heritage, social relations and Black institutions. Nineteenth century Black intellectuals and community activists were the vanguards of a 'Black movement' that sought to invoke and foster a doctrine of Black pride, self-determination, economic solidarity, academic achievement and other forms of individual and collective Black action. This nineteenth century Black intellectual/activist movement was the wellspring from which Black Victorian Feminists emerged. African American women, Black Victorian Feminists in particular, were essential contributors to and participants in this intellectual/ activist movement. While they were thoroughly committed to the goals and aspirations of the movement, Black Victorian Feminists added their own goals and aspirations to the agenda—the elevation of Black womanhood.

The uniqueness of African American women's experience, in part, revolves around the fact that Black women are historically positioned at the nexus of two of the most well developed ideologies in America: being woman and being Black.[12] During the Slaveocracy, the enslaved Black woman's chattel status, sex and race combined to create a complicated set of myths about Black womanhood. By the late nineteenth century, a legacy of sexual exploitation and the conflation of illicit sexuality and promiscuity to Black womanhood formed the ideological underpinnings of demeaning, controlling images of African American women. The quest, by Black women, for respect, dignity and economic and educational opportunity was undermined by these pervasive negative stereotypes of Black womanhood.

While African American women had battled against the damaging and demeaning stereotypes of their womanhood since the dark days of the Slaveocracy, their efforts of identity re-clamation and re-formation primarily operated from behind a protective veil of secrecy. In the late nineteenth century, a cadre of Black women intellectuals and activists boldly and bravely stepped forward to fill the 'public space' left empty of alternate representations of Black women's lives with hitherto private positive and empowering images. They devised and implemented a plan of action whose purpose was to realize the goal of the elevation of Black womanhood. I call these women Black Victorian Feminists. I apply the complex and contradictory title of Black Victorian Feminist to these women for several reasons. The term Victorian denotes a particular lifestyle and ideal that these women adhered to and advocated. Black Victorian Feminists appropriated and subverted white Victorian ideals of 'traditional' gender roles, views on sexuality, and middle class sentiment, modified them and then integrated them into their re-formative efforts. I deliberately apply the contemporary term Black feminist to these nineteenth century women in order to emphasize and better conceptualize the fact that Black Victorian Feminist ideology was rooted in an identity re-claimation that was both radical and libratory.

The methodology of my analysis of Black women's participation at the Exposition revolves around one multifaceted endeavor—to shift the paradigm of 'traditional' American history through developing new categories—telling a new story. While there is a considerable body of literature about the presence of African Americans in the Columbian Exposition, there has been very little written about their presence as being an example of the "…transcendence of black human agency in the face of external constraints."[13] In *All the World is Here!: The Black Presence at White City* (2000), Christopher Reed posits that the traditional paradigm of cultural movements confers primacy to protest movements that mount overt challenges to oppression. Such a paradigm positions conflict and protest as essential components in the forward progression of cultural movements. Yet the primacy of this paradigm ignores the importance of sustained daily resistance—an alternate method of human agency, and a mainstay in Black women's history.

How can historians truly and fully investigate Black women's experience if they primarily do so through consideration of what the larger society permitted or prohibited African American women to do? "Measuring black progress through the prism of what was forbidden by whites, of what allegedly couldn't be accomplished because of impediments imposed by the white world, fails miserably as a comprehensive tool for understanding given the level of human agency evinced by African Americans throughout American history."[14] It is not my intention to portray the major and minor roles that Black women have played in American history as greater or more important than the many other groups of people that make up vital parts of the 'American whole.' It is my intention to re-examine the existing historical record through the gaze of a historically invisible group in American history. I contend that in order to fully explore and understand the existence of Black women's distinct history, and its indivisibility from American history, it is essential that Black women's differential experience be viewed in terms of interests, privileges, deprivations, and a self-defined standpoint.[15]

'Traditional' American history is inherently the history of Western Civilization. In this story "…the privileged subject is white and male, usually a member of the ruling elite, and the social relationships that sustain this privilege [are] rarely, if ever, examined."[16] As a result the existing framework of investigation is one where the "…Euro (andro-) centric viewpoint is embedded in categories of analysis, in notions of historical significance, in beliefs about who the important actors are, and in the causal logic of the story."[17] Within this paradigm all non-Europeans, all women, the poor, and all intersecting subsets of these identity variables appear to be relegated to the role of victim and loser. Conversely, the placement of the privileged white male (and sometimes white female) as the protagonists in the American story establishes white as not merely a skin color (a problematic construct in itself) but the *norm* from which all Black women *deviate*. It is in this way that Black women's history may be integrated into and *still remain marginal within the scope of American history.*

I intend to place Black women in the role of protagonist in this story. My goal is to not merely displace the relegation of Black women as deviants from the norm but to create a fresh framework where a Black feminist viewpoint is embedded in categories of analysis, in notions of historical significance, in beliefs about who the important actors are, and in the causal logic of the story. Utilizing this method of analysis I intend to historicize how the identity variables of race, gender, and class did not exist independently of each other, nor compete for supremacy, but overlapped, intersected, and reinforced each other, thus I will create a fresh framework from which to locate, and better understand, how Black women's history and experience exists as an *identifiable socio-historical process.*

Moreover, I will shift the traditional historical paradigm that deems the records of African American women suspect or non-authentic *because* they are Black women's records: "To legitimize black women's history, black women historians, in particular, were put in the ironic and untenable position of having to be especially careful to corroborate black women's sources with those of whites and black men—the very source material that made black women invisible in the first place."[18] Instead, I intend to locate my examination firmly on this nineteenth century Black feminist discourse and intellectual enterprise. These women were addressing the monumental changes occurring within and without the Black women's community thirty years after the end of slavery and that is where I intend to focus my historical gaze. I do not intend to *compare* nineteenth century Black feminist discourse and intellectual enterprise to that of nineteenth century white men, white women, and/or Black men. Nor will I *contrast* Black women's history to women's history or American history. In a fundamental way the nineteenth century Black woman's experience was *not* an extreme case of what women experienced as a group in America. Black women did not experience sexism the same way white women did, nor did they experience racism in the same way that Black men did. Owing to the combination of color and their sex, Black women were exploited differently than either white women or Black men. Nineteenth century Black women's experience was born of the *simultaneous manifestations* of racism and sexism, not an extreme form of one or the other. Such an understanding creates a new language that expresses the unique nature of the experience of nineteenth century African American women. The focus of this dissertation is precise. I contend that, in this instance, Black women's history and experience stand-alone.

Moreover, I intend to illustrate, that what renders late nineteenth century Black feminist discourse an intellectual enterprise is the 'coming together' of several crucial factors: the larger society's construction and maintenance of damaging, derogatory stereotypes of Black womanhood; the reality of Black women's lives, during and after the Slaveocracy[19]; Black women's reliance on their own standards in the development of a self-defined image; a triad of oppression; and an insurgent nineteenth century 'Black movement'. These women engaged in the further development of a distinct Black feminist discourse that is, consequently, an important yet largely overlooked chapter in Women's History and American History.

2

PROGRESSIONS

True progress is never made by spasms. Real progress is growth. It must begin in the seed. Then, 'first the blade, then the ear, after that the full corn in the ear'...the black woman of to-day stands mute and wondering at the Herculean task devolving upon her. But cycles wait for her. No other hand can move the lever. She must be loosed from her hands and set to work.

—Anna Julia Cooper,
*Womanhood: A Vital Element in the Regeneration and Progress
of a Race*

The genesis of Black feminist consciousness, discourse, and intellectual enterprise originated in the lived experiences that African women brought with them to North America. On slave ships "they came from African villages, cities, and states that had various social rules and in which they played diverse roles...They were part of societies with rich and longstanding heritages in which women were traders, agriculturalists, weavers, warriors, leaders, and especially mothers."[20] At the outset, it is important to remember that Africans and African Americans were *women and men of distinct cultures and civilizations before they had the denigrating identity of "Slave" assigned to them.* Ironically, enslavement encouraged Black women to adapt key elements of their African legacy and utilize them as one of the tools needed to maintain their individual identities. The Slaveocracy also modified the evolution of Black feminist discourse and intellectual enterprise—out of the horrors of slavery a distinct African American women's culture and community was born. In order to better contextualize nineteenth century Black Victorian Feminist discourse and intellectual enterprise, this chapter will explore the genesis of African American feminism through an examination of the exterior reality of Black women's experience under the Slaveocratic regime—the institutionalization of the degradation, dehumanization and defeminization of enslaved Black women; the interior reality of this experience—the enslaved women's community; and the alternative reality of this experience—free African Americans and free African American women in Antebellum America, and Black Victorian Feminists and their efforts at identity re-clamation and re-formation.

Exterior Realities: The Slaveocracy (or the Antebellum Period)

She was counted but little higher than the brute creation that surrounded her, and was said to possess neither a brain nor a soul. Scourged by the hard hand of the slave-driver, and suffering every privation, there fell upon her a helplessness born of despair; but with an implicit trust and unswerving faith in God, she caught the glinting light from the peak of freedom's day.

—Hallie Quinn Brown,
The Organized Efforts of the Colored Women of the South to Improve Their Condition

The exterior reality of the Slaveocracy, for enslaved Black women, revolved around the systematic degradation, dehumanization and defeminization of enslaved women by the Slaveocratic regime. The dehumanistic mechanism of the Slaveocracy is best characterized by the conflation of enslavement to 'social death'. "A slave could not make contracts, own property, or form legal partnerships on his or her own. By law the slave had no brother or sister, no husband or wife, no son or daughter, no ancestors and no posterity...the slave was cut off from society, making slavery itself a form of social death...slavery's essence rested on the degrading exclusion of the slave from all public life."[21] The relegation of the 'slave' to such a 'social death' not only effectively severed the enslaved community's formal ties to the larger society, it also abetted enslavers' claim to property rights over the lives and livelihoods of those they enslaved. Through legal, cultural, social and religious means enslaved African Americans were denied even the title of human and labeled, and treated, as chattel—inanimate objects, pieces of property: "...slaves could be alienated—bought and sold, bequeathed and inherited, won or lost."[22]

The socio-cultural construction of the idealized 'slave woman' was a direct result of American society's attempt to reconcile and *rationalize* enslaved women's existence with prevalent constructions of idealized gender and racial roles, and religious attitudes. The most essential element of reconciliation/rationalization, besides the dehumanistic mechanisms of the Slaveocratic regime, revolved around the systematic *defeminization* of enslaved Black women. It is true that gender and race ideologies predate those of the United States. Nevertheless, it was during the Slaveocracy that these ideologies were molded into a distinct American mythology. Deborah Gray White posits that the uniqueness of Black woman's experience is that she is positioned at the nexus of two of the most well developed ideologies in America: being woman and being Black. During the Slaveocracy, the enslaved woman's chattel status, sex, and race combined to create a complicated set of myths about Black womanhood. In *Ar'n't I A Woman: Female Slaves in the Plantation South* (1985), White examines the primary impetus for nineteenth century Black women's continuing reconstruction of their womanhood—persistent, damaging and denigrating stereotypes of Black womanhood. White locates two subsets that form the ideological underpinnings for the derogatory image(s) of African American women—Jezebel and Mammy.

Governed entirely by her libido, Jezebel was the counter image of the Victorian lady. The idealized antebellum Victorian lady was naturally meek and submissive, weaker in intellect and physical strength than men, more pious than men and ever virginal. Her main goal in life was to get married, nurture her children, gently guide but not nag her husband, tend to an immaculate household and happily take a secondary role in family and community life—the man was the leader, the woman the silent follower. Jezebel, on the other hand: "…did not lead men and children to God: piety was foreign to her. She saw no advantage in prudery, indeed domesticity paled before matters of the flesh."[23] The roots of Jezebel are found in Africa when Europeans were first exposed to Africans. Semi-nudity in a tropical climate was labeled as lewdness and cultural traditions like polygamy, for example, were attributed to Africans' inability to control their supposedly "powerfully lustful urges."[24] In the United States Black women's lives under the Slaveocracy created situations that seemingly confirmed European views of enslaved women's supposed natural and immutable lustful, lascivious urges. There were four 'situations' in particular that White points to that seemingly confirmed and furthered American views of Black women's unfitness for true womanhood: fecundity, the auction block, life on the plantation, and coerced sex and/or outright rape. Major periodicals of the day carried articles detailing optimal conditions under which enslaved women would reproduce and discussion of the merits of a particular *'breeder'* was considered appropriate dinner conversation. On the auction block slave buyers routinely exposed Black women's bodies and kneaded their stomachs to determine how many children a slave would be capable of producing—all situations antithetical to western gender conventions.[25]

Perhaps the most disturbing aspect of the enslaved woman's experience was her confrontation with sexual coercion and/or outright rape. When faced with the worst experience the Slaveocracy had to offer it is not surprising that some enslaved women opted to trade sexual 'favors' to those that enslaved, abused, and exploited them, in return for food and/or respite from hard labor and the lash, and/or the procurement of a measure of safety for their children. One of the despicable aspects of the sexual abuse and exploitation that enslaved women had to sometimes resist/sometimes endure was what was known as the "Fancy Trade,"—the sale of light-skinned Black women as prostitutes and concubines.[26] Ironically, the realities of fecundity, the auction block, life on the plantation, coerced sex and outright rape were situations that enslaved women negotiated and survived, to the best of their ability, but they *were not of their creation or under their control*. Nevertheless, Black women carried the blame; blame assigned to them by the true culprits. The rationalization was that white men never had to use their authority or violence to obtain sex from enslaved Black women. "Whether or not slave women desired such relationships with white men was immaterial, the conventional wisdom was that black women were naturally promiscuous, and thus, desired such connections."[27]

The sexual exploitation of enslaved women, cloaked in the Jezebel myth, was further rationalized and justified through pro-slavery proponents' claim that the sexual exploitation of Black women further championed the cult of true womanhood. Black women acted as a 'buffer' that kept Southern white women free and pure from the taint of immorality. But the myth of Jezebel simultaneously caused a troubling rift in the ideology of the Slaveocracy. The proponents of slavery could no longer afford to ignore Northern and abolitionist charges that in such a degenerative climate Southern white women could hardly be true Victorian 'ladies' and yet be in such close proximity, day and night, to such purportedly sexually immoral Black women. No matter how Jezebel was cast, rationalized, and/or lauded "…implicit in the argument was an admission of impropriety, namely that black women were indeed kept in a state of prostitution by white men who had little incentive to exercise self-control,"[28] thus, an alternate image of Black women needed to be created; one that simultaneously championed true womanhood, white moral supremacy, and the justness of slavery—Mammy.

Selected for her worth, reliability, and righteousness, the mythical Mammy was the woman who could do anything and do it better than anyone else. Always motherly, her very title was steeped in maternal sentiment. While the mythical Jezebel was nubile, the mythical Mammy was elderly and fat. White posits that Mammy's advanced age and large size might be a metaphor for the asexuality attributed to her. Among Anglo American Protestant middle and upper classes, the Victorian maternal ideal was understood in terms of asexuality. Thus old age and a large girth put Mammy beyond carnality and sensuality—through Mammy, Jezebel was made chaste. She was, purportedly, a domestic goddess, so respected, revered, and obeyed by all that she served as friend and advisor to the master and mistress. Mammy was the personification of the ideal slave and the ideal woman. Yet Mammy, hence all Black women, could never be (or become) a 'true woman'. Mammy was allowed into this idealized white womanhood only to the extent that she served her enslavers. It is important to remember, however, that the South (and America at large) did not abandon the Jezebel myth. Rather, Jezebel and Mammy were inverse stereotypes that existed simultaneously. *Both images were accepted and utilized depending on the convenience and the context of thought*: "On the one hand there was the woman obsessed with matters of the flesh, on the other was the asexual woman. One was carnal, the other maternal. One was at heart a slut, the other was deeply religious. One was Jezebel, the other a Mammy…They are black images but being almost as old as the images of Eve and the Virgin Mary, they are also universal female archetypes." [29] Although White's early work facilitates the de-construction of the *exterior* construction of Black womanhood, to examine the experience of African American women, through the gaze of the oppressor, underneath the rubric of the traditional historical paradigm obfuscates the examination of the *interior* aspects of Black women's distinct experience and self-defined standpoint.

Interior Realities: An Enslaved Woman's Point of View

The majority of our women are not heroines…It is enough for me to know that while in the eyes of the highest tribunal in America she was deemed no more than a chattel, an irresponsible thing, a dull block, to be drawn hither or thither at the volition of an owner, the Afro-American woman maintained ideals of womanhood unshamed by any ever conceived.

—Anna Julia Cooper,
*The Intellectual Progress of the Colored Women of the United States
Since the Emancipation Proclamation*

In "Female Slaves: Sex Roles and Status in the Antebellum South" (1984) Deborah Gray White explores the interior reality of the enslaved Black women's community—one they themselves participated in creating and maintaining. White focuses on what Black women could do, and did, in a distinct community that existed and thrived in the slave quarters, the 'Big House,' and in the fields. She locates and explores enslaved women's self-reliance and self-sufficiency through an examination of some of their activities. More importantly, however, she discusses the implications of enslaved women's actions in their community and the probable impact on women's status in slave society.[30] White begins her investigation with the observation that enslaved women did a variety of heavy and dirty labor.[31] "They [enslaved women] planted, weeded, and harvested crops, and during the winter months they burned brush, cleared pasture, mended fences and repaired equipment…a slaveowner just as "naturally" put his bondswomen to work chopping cotton as washing, ironing, or cooking…Together with their fathers, husbands, brothers, and sons, black women spent up to fourteen hours a day toiling out of doors; often under a blazing sun."[32] But they might have also gained some intangibles from doing the same work as men. Anthropologists Leith Mullings and Karen Sacks, have demonstrated that in societies where men and women are engaged in the production of the same kinds of goods and where property was not a factor, participation in production gives women freedom and independence.[33] Thus, since neither enslaved men nor women had access to, or control over, the fruits of their labor, equality in the fields may have encouraged egalitarianism in the enslaved Black community.

As for domestic work and enslaved women, 'women's work' took on a particular meaning, unorthodox to the traditional ideology of domesticity. Some 'woman's work' required skills that were highly valued and even coveted because a valued skill could purchase a higher position in the social echelons of the 'slave world' and ease some of the plights of enslavement. For example, good cooks were highly respected in both the Black and white communities. Sewing, too, could be a lucrative skill, especially if an enslaved woman sewed for the slave owner's family; sometimes these women were hired out and allowed to keep a portion of the profit. A few enslaved women were able to accumulate enough profit to buy their own and their family's freedom.[34] Additionally, Midwifery and/or 'doctoring' were important occupations.

In support of her contention of the existence of a distinct enslaved woman's community, White notes that an important aspect of both specialized and mundane woman's work was frequently performed in all female groups. Such a situation provided enslaved women the opportunity to control many aspects of their world and allowed them to rank and order themselves vis-à-vis one another, in a manner not aligned with either Black men, white men or white women. Claire

Robertson and Nancy Tanner have postulated that in societies where women are not isolated from one another and/or placed under a man's authority; where women cooperated in the performance of household tasks; where their roles were usually complementary to those of men, and the female world existed independently of the male world, women, by necessity and design, were prone to be more self-sufficient.[35] These elements of the enslaved woman's community may be an indication that Black women were not inferior to their male counterparts. Instead, the existence of this distinct community allowed enslaved Black women to obtain a sense of self, which was *apart from the larger enslaved community and the Slaveocratic classes.*

White discusses another aspect of the enslaved woman's experience that was quite different from Black men, white men, and white women: matrimony. Unlike white women, enslaved women did not receive traditional marriage benefits (i.e. property or essentials like food, clothing, or shelter). Furthermore, within the marital realm itself, other than denying legal, social, or religious sanction or recognition of the institution of marriage, the selling of children, and barring sexual coercion and/or outright rape,—which I contend actually nourished a resistant, survival oriented distinct Black woman's community and consciousness—white men did not usually interfere in the daily activities and chores of familial life. Black men, by circumstance of their perpetual servitude, were unable to bestow traditional marriage benefits upon their wives and families and the practice of 'marrying abroad' (having a spouse on a different plantation) could only have reinforced this situation. When men live apart from women they cannot control them. In almost all societies where men consistently control women, that control is based on male ownership and distribution of property and/or control of certain culturally valued subsistence goods. These circumstances had to contribute to female self-sufficiency and independence from enslaved men, their captors, and intensified female intradependancy—hence strengthening the enslaved woman's community, as well as strengthening self-reliance in the face of the brutal horrors of the Slaveocracy.[36]

If enslaved Black women did not receive traditional marital benefits, yet we know that Black families did exist and even flourish during the Slaveocracy, how did the Black family function? White offers a term and concept, in explanation, that also serves to further debunk the myth of the Black matriarch: the enslaved Black family was *matrifocal. Matrifocality* is a term that conveys the fact that women "...in their role as mothers are the focus of familial relationships."[37] It *does not* mean that fathers were absent or emasculated. Rather, the mother becomes the focal point of familial activity; she is more central than the father to the family's continuity and survival as a unit. The most important factor is *the supremacy of the mother-child bond above all other relationships.* Deborah Gray White explores the interior reality of the enslaved Black woman's community. Within this community she locates one of the sites of Black women's self-reliance and self-sufficiency through an examination of some of their activities—focusing on what enslaved women could do and did. Out of the 'equality' of slavery, Black women were able to initiate and shape an intellectualized standpoint about their circumstance and create distinct models of behavior from which they could facilitate a means of individual and group identity.

In "Gender Convention, Ideals, and Identity Among Antebellum Virginia Slave Women" (1996), Brenda E. Stevenson explores some of the positive images that enslaved women created of, and for, themselves; images that actively proved false Jezebel and Mammy. Enslaved women's autobiographies convey much about what they expressed as their requisite concerns and responsibilities within the boundaries of their oppressed world. Their autobiographies establish a basic premise of slave women's morality and purpose—the protection and survival of Black life. Furthermore, the *prerogative* of the enslaved woman was the protection and survival of Black life *in the face of white opposition*, thus constructing a Black women's identity that is complex and oppositional. Through the 'vehicle of the autobiographical story' enslaved women were able to construct what, for them, was an operative, legitimate identity, a 'counterimage' to the larger culture's construction of demeaning stereotypes of Black womanhood.[38] There are numerous stories, for example, about the rape and physical abuse that enslaved women endured. Most of these women could not fight back, except perhaps in the *testimony* of their painful stories—which vindicated their assertion of sexual morality. Those women who did fight back, and win, emerged in the lore and mythology of enslaved women—both as models for Black women's conduct and symbols of resistance that engendered a sense of pride. Enslaved women's image(s) of themselves were overwhelmingly positive, even heroic. Enslaved women described themselves, and their peers, as self-reliant and self-determined survivalists who, sometimes overtly, sometimes covertly, resisted the tyranny of the Slaveocratic regime.

Furthermore, enslaved women viewed their defiant thoughts and acts of resistance as *characteristics* of womanhood. Resistance to the horrors and indignities of slavery helped them to maintain "their most fundamental claims to womanhood; that is, their female sexuality and physicality, and their roles as mothers, nurturers, and wives."[39] Most enslaved children grew up in households with only their mothers present on a daily basis. It was their *mothers* who had to make the day-to-day decisions that fashioned their lives. Enslaved children's mothers, and other women of the slave community, provided whatever protection and support enslaved children received. Women, in their role as mother, were the stabilizing forces in slave families and communities. Tragically, the majority of enslaved mothers were not able to protect their children from the most devastating consequences of enslavement—physical and psychological beatings, sexual abuse, and permanent separation from family and loved ones. Nor could they risk further harm, to themselves or their families, by publicly criticizing the slaveholding men and women who were the perpetrators of such atrocities.

Stevenson also points to the fact that enslaved women not only constructed a self-defined identity, *they also developed characterizations of, and about, slaveholding white women.* While white America mythologized the elite white woman as the model of femininity for the world to emulate, Black women relied upon their own standards. The white cultural construction of a gendered dichotomy of separate spheres was not a reality for enslaved people. For enslaved women idealized notions of female passivity and helplessness were *absurd!* Black women were keenly aware of, and had definite opinions about, the privileged and *purposeful* behavior of white women and found such behavior incompatible with the larger society's avowals of middle and upper class white women's religious and moral superiority. "As mistress of the house she was the master's delegate, his implementer. They [white women] might deplore their men's excessive drinking, sexual philandering, and abuse of power, but they rarely rejected the system that established their sense of personal identity within a solid community."[40]

Enslaved women's autobiographical accounts, as presented in Stevenson's essay, are provocative for several reasons. They presuppose Black women's ability to intellectualize their experience—from a distinct community and consciousness—and to implicate the inhuman actions of white men and women. Stevenson reminds us that while the larger society created an image of Black women, *Black women created their own images*—viable, proud self-images that helped them to evade the dehumanization and de-feminization of slavery. Cultural identity and consciousness is crucially connected to memory and reality. It is a matter of *becoming* as well as *being* for the narrator. It comes as no surprise, then, that there are so many exemplary and heroic women found in the autobiographical stories of, in this instance, Virginia ex-slave women. Heroism, self-reliance, and willfulness—in the face of such brutal social conditions became, *especially important characteristics in enslaved women's self-identity.* The combination of ideals incumbent in the self-images of enslaved women, actively created in their verbal and written texts—a survivalist, self-determined philosophy—comprised a system of morality, a morality founded on the continuation of Black life, humanity, and femininity *within*, and in opposition to those *without* who threatened this continuation.

Alternative Realities: Free African Americans in Antebellum America

In this arena then is to be the last death struggle of political tyranny, of religious bigotry, and intellectual intolerance, of caste illiberality and class exclusiveness. And the last monster that shall be throttled forever methinks is race prejudice.

—Anna Julia Cooper, *Has America a Race Problem?*

While the Slaveocracy thrived, there too existed a free African American community in the south and the north. This community primarily consisted of emancipated and manumitted slaves, "There was also a small amount of immigration from abroad…"[41] By the onset of the nineteenth century, more than 100,000 free African Americans resided in the United States.[42] Like most nineteenth century Americans, free African Americans believed in, and expected to be participants in, achieving the 'American Dream' "—a compound of beliefs in the possibility (indeed, the likelihood) of achieving freedom, individual economic success, and personal, institutional, and societal improvement."[43] Sadly, however, free African Americans living in antebellum America were continually confronted with the fact that the larger society had deemed them to be ineligible for participation in the endeavor to attain the 'American Dream'. "Because they were black, freedom was always and everywhere for them cruelly incomplete."[44] If they were to lay claim to the 'American Dream', free African Americans would have to gain it *in spite of the larger society.*

The manifestations of racial prejudice, discrimination and oppression experienced by free African Americans nationwide, were varied. Nevertheless, one factor remained constant—its universality. Antebellum free African Americans were pigeonholed as a distinct and *undesirable* 'under-class' by the larger society. This outcast status affected every aspect of free Black existence—employment opportunities, or lack thereof, public life, education and religious worship—all were experienced through the prism of prejudice, discrimination, and oppression. Free African Americans seeking employment opportunities, for example, found strong opposition from the larger community at almost every turn. African Americans faced the strongest opposition when they attempted to enter artisan trades.[45] White journeymen and apprentices refused to work with African Americans, assuming that the aspiring Black apprentice could find a master that was willing to teach them. For those seeking menial (or unskilled) employment (i.e. coal miners or street pavers) "...even the most laborious and least profitable occupations, prejudice and pride pursued the free persons of color."[46] Free African Americans seeking occupational opportunities found respite from wholesale exclusion in only the least remunerative jobs (i.e. laundress, ragpicker, and/or chimney sweep). Thus, the vast majority of free African Americans remained trapped at the very bottom of the economic ladder.

Ironically, occupational diversity and employment opportunity for free African Americans living in the antebellum south were much more extensive than for free African Americans living in the antebellum north. Leonard Curry posits that two factors provide a clearer understanding of this phenomenon. Firstly, from the beginning, continuing to the end, of the Slaveocracy "...slaves had always been extensively employed as skilled workers...Hence, by the antebellum era southern whites did not perceive black artisans as either strange or threatening elements..."[47] In addition, the presence of Black artisans greatly increased the likelihood that aspiring free Black artisans would be able to procure apprenticeship positions that would, in turn, enable them to enter their chosen trades. Secondly, the antebellum free Black communities of the south were largely the by-products of selective manumission, not mass emancipation. "...many earned the money to buy their freedom, some were freed as a reward for their labor or loyalty, [or] because of familial relationships with their masters."[48] Thus, Curry contends, the free southern Black communities were populated with the highest percentage of the most "...talented of the slave population, while many others had familial ties that were likely to make it easier for them to acquire education, training and capital."[49]

The social, economic and political position of free African Americans was intimately informed, and diligently controlled, by the larger community's use of dejure and defacto discrimination. Most southern states required free African Americans to carry 'certificates of freedom' on their persons at all times. If they did not they could be "...held in jail...some were eventually sold back into slavery."[50] In many southern jurisdictions free African Americans were required to register with the local police or have a white 'guardian.' African Americans could not vote, serve on juries or testify against white defendants in a court of law. Additionally, in many southern states, free African Americans were subjected to "...mandatory curfews, an end to free assembly, and exclusion from schools as well as many trades and occupations."[51] Free African Americans found little, if any, respite in the northwestern and/or western sections of the antebellum United States for many of these so called 'Black laws' existed to the exact letter and sentiment as those of the south. These hostile and humiliating laws forced many free African Americans to flee to the northeast, where Black oppression still existed but was not founded in law but in social convention.

To be a free, or enslaved, African American in antebellum America was to be a member of an outcast community. Moreover, this community was viewed and treated by the larger society as not only inferior but also *sub-human*. Consequently, it is no wonder that free African Americans were the recipients, for the most part, of little better treatment at the hand of the larger society than their enslaved brethren. "Around any corner and down any street—at work, at play, or at prayer [they] were apt to be met by curses, missiles, and physical assault."[52] Of course many free African Americans, especially those in an urban environment, were able to avoid assaults and public exclusion but only through meticulous conformity to discriminatory and degrading social custom. Those free African Americans who were able to obtain a 'peaceful' life did so by avoiding certain areas of the cities and towns in which they lived and through cultivation of a 'servile and submissive' mien and carriage when encountering members of the larger society. Free African Americans knew that they had only their wits and each other upon which to rely. They would find little or no respite from the 'white' world:

> "...not one sentient black in antebellum America could escape the knowledge that he lived in a white land under a white government that administered white law for the benefit of a white population, and that in the eyes of all these he was a being inferior to all but the most base and degraded of whites, and that no amount of conformity to white mores and customs or acceptance of white values could change that reality."[53]

Ironically, it was the larger society's rabid obsession with white superiority and Black inferiority, the equally rabid need of the larger society to segregate, subordinate, discriminate and humiliate all African Americans, and the larger society's "...duplicity, hypocrisy, mendacity, and faithlessness to the elements and implications of its own vaunted creed"[54] that provided an essential element in the coalescence of a free African American community.

In antebellum America, whether African Americans desired it or not, Blackness was the central and overriding consideration in their lives. The larger society had deemed, and were able to enforce, that Blackness would determine where Black people would live, where they were buried, where they worshiped, where they worked and where they spent their money. It seemed inevitable that free African Americans would form a physical and psychic Black community that would span geographical areas and encompass a myriad of life experiences under the umbrella of one national identity. The larger society may have established, and stridently maintained, the exterior elements of the free Black community. The details, however, the nooks and crannies, if you will, emerged from deep within this community. There are three sites, in particular, that formed the nucleus of the interior, self-created, roots of the free antebellum Black community: the church, associational activities, and the modes in which African Americans protested the 'exterior' yoke of discrimination and oppression by the larger society.

During the American Colonial era religious congregations were interracial. By the onset of the Slaveocracy the unavoidable reality of the adversarial nature of Black and white relations made the separation of congregations, along racial lines, inevitable. On the one hand, white church leaders and congregationalists were unable to deny or ignore, if only to themselves, the blatant hypocrisy sorely evident between their religious creed and their individual prejudices and depravities: "Religion, like every other force in America, was first used as an instrument and servant of slavery. All attempts to Christianize the 'negro' were limited by the fact that he was property of a valuable and peculiar sort, and that the property value must not be disturbed...Do not open the Bible too wide."[55]

On the other hand, as the numbers of *free* Black church leaders and congregationalists grew, they became increasingly unwilling to mutely accept "...discriminations which they had seen as inevitable concomitants of their [former] servile status, but which they now perceived with greater clarity as springing from distinctions based on race not condition."[56] Free African Americans were continually subjected to pervasive prejudice and discrimination—in every section of the country and in every religious denomination. If free African Americans were to ever achieve true religious freedom, foster community development and identification they would have to establish churches that were "...the vision of the black spirit, organized by black minds, built by black hands, and the solace of black souls."[57] Thus, the first half of the nineteenth century saw the establishment of the African Methodist Episcopal Church, the African Methodist Episcopal Zion Church, and the African Union Church. In addition to these major Black churches, free African Americans established small congregations of Baptist, Presbyterian, Dutch Reformed, Lutheran and Catholic faiths. By 1850 there were over 100 separate Black religious congregations that operated primarily in the north: "In a world where every lever of power was held by a white hand and every symbol of authority was white, the separated church stood as a towering monument to the zeal, strength, and determination of the American Negro—a black rock casting a cooling shadow in a harsh desert of whiteness."[58]

Thus, the Black Church became an essential fortifying staple for the African American community. "Truly African American in its origins, it provided a spiritual cohesiveness that permitted its people to absorb, interpret, and practice the Christian faith—to make it their own...[the Black Church] promoted a sense of individual and collective worth and perpetuated the belief in human dignity that countered the racist preachings of the master class."[59] The Black Church represented the physical, psychic and spiritual center of the Black community, in part, by operating as a 'public sphere'. Although African Americans in the north were nominally free the larger society continued to deny them access to public accommodations (i.e. parks, libraries, and restaurants). *Regardless of individual denominations*, Black churches operated as a public space, for both secular and religious groups, in the Black community. Black churches housed a dizzying variety of programs that catered to the Black community: "...schools, circulating libraries, concerts, restaurants, insurance companies, vocational training, athletic clubs...held political rallies, clubwomen's conferences, and school graduations. It was the one space truly accessible to the black community."[60] The Black Church, too, operating as a public sphere provided the much needed space for African Americans to meet, discuss and debate issues important to the community and then disseminate new ideas throughout the larger Black community.

Pervasive discrimination and oppression, coupled with the desire to achieve the 'American Dream', provided the impetus for free African Americans to pool their resources and utilize cooperative action to socially and economically advance their community. The larger society's attempts to limit educational and occupational opportunities of African Americans meant that those of the Black community were largely unable to acquire property or establish financial resources. Therefore, the earliest Black associational societies were primarily benevolent and beneficial societies. Benevolent societies collected donations from more affluent African Americans and then dispensed aid and funds to assist the poor. Beneficial societies organized the limited resources of the poor and the working poor for mutual support.

While the movement to establish mutual aid societies spread rapidly in the black community, the first half of the nineteenth century saw the largest growth of these societies. Naturally, Black men who had the same or similar occupations often formed their own beneficial societies. In 1830, for example, Black coachmen, porters and mechanics founded societies in Philadelphia and Baltimore.

During that same decade, Black barbers, brick makers and caulkers established mutual aid societies. The poorest members of the Black community, too, formed mutual aid societies, though their sense of unity did not necessarily spring from job identification. Instead they were united by "...their deprivation, their foresight, and their blackness."[61]

The benevolent and mutual aid societies established and maintained by free African Americans played five crucial roles within the burgeoning free Black community. First it provided strength in numbers—these societies empowered African Americans to accomplish as a group what many could not as individuals. Second experience, participation in these societies provided their members with the experiential tools essential for institutional development. Third, opportunity for interaction—these societies provided African Americans the opportunity to socialize in a private and *safe* environment. Fourth, a sense of belonging—participation gave members a recognized place that afforded them a voice and *respect*. And lastly, fostering a sense of community—the members of these societies "...created structures around which coalesced meaningful sub societies and from which radiated filaments of social consciousness which eventually formed themselves into a tenuous fragile web of community."[62]

Armed with tools acquired in building a Black Church and Black organizations, leaders in the community began to build another important institution—schools. Leaders and 'common folk' alike understood that true and lasting individual and communal advancement would only be accomplished through personal and collective high levels of literacy and intellectual development. Many believed that while the vast majority of African Americans could not claim family influence or personal wealth as conduits to achieve prosperity, education would prove to be the great equalizer. As with nearly every other aspect of antebellum Black life the larger society either completely banned Black enrollment in public schools or severely limited Black access and level of achievement. Thus, the Black community mobilized and established and maintained their own 'public schools'. Black public schools fell into three categories: entrepreneurial, institutional or philanthropic. Entrepreneurial schools were schools where the parents of each student paid a tuition that covered all costs (i.e. teachers salaries, books and supplies). At Institutional schools churches and other community organizations "...provided quarters for the school and sometimes guaranteed the salary of the instructor, though tuition was usually charged..."[63] Philanthropic schools were organized and funded by sympathetic members of the larger society. They rarely charged fees to those who were unable to pay but they "...usually admitted students without reference to their ability or willingness to meet tuition charges."[64]

With an emphasis on developing literacy, Black schools taught large numbers of Black adults to read and write. Just as important, however, was the commitment to provide Black children and adults with a public primary school curriculum comparable to that of white public schools. Moreover, many of these schools were equally dedicated to providing advanced courses in such subjects as languages and philosophy. Sadly, even with an education, better access to lucrative employment opportunity was still denied to most African Americans. The color barrier was too resolute. Nevertheless, the creation and maintenance of schools significantly contributed to the further coalescence of the Black community, and the majority of African Americans "…never lost faith in the individual and community values of education."[65]

Free African Americans living in antebellum America lived, and negotiated, in a dangerous time in history. Daily, and in myriads of ways, they dealt with racial prejudice and discrimination, oppression and humiliation, verbal and physical assault, and the denial of even the most basic rights of American citizenship. In the midst of this truly scary environment, free African Americans persevered and laid the foundation of a distinct Black community. This community coalesced, found a tentative footing, and addressed the economic, educational and occupational barriers to personal and communal social, political and cultural advancement. In conjunction with the coalescence of the free Black community leaders and 'common folk' began to voice, with increasing eloquence and volume, their objection to the greatest obstacle facing each and every African American living in antebellum America—slavery.

> "We [African Americans] were classed as goods and chattel, and numbered on our master's ledgers with horses, sheep and swine. We were subject to barter and sale, and could be bequeathed and inherited at will, like real estate and any other property. In the language of the law: A slave was one in the power of his master to whom he belonged. He could acquire nothing, own nothing that did not belong to his master. His time and talents, his mind and muscle, his body and soul, were the property of his master. He, with all that could be predicted of him as a human being, was simply the property of his master. He was a marketable commodity …a beast of burden.[66]

While the intricacies of prejudice and discrimination had clear detrimental effects on the Black quest for the 'American Dream', nothing rankled more than the continued existence of slavery. Slavery, and the Slaveocracy, was the most physically, psychologically, and spiritually damaging factor in nineteenth century Black existence. The burgeoning free Black community knew this and did everything in their power to fight, hamper and eradicate the institution of slavery. While those who could fought against the horror embodied in the Slaveocracy from its inception, it was not until the first decades of the nineteenth century that African Americans began to organize as a community around the cause of abolition. In 1836 in Boston a group of free African Americans formed the General Colored Association of Massachusetts. Soon thereafter, the African Abolition Free-Hold Society and the African Female Anti-Slavery Society were formed. By 1840 similar societies had been formed in New York, Philadelphia, Pittsburgh and Providence. "Additionally, numerous vigorous condemnations of slavery emanated from urban black meetings and from individual Negro residents of the nation's major cities, growing ever harsher throughout the half-century."[67]

Free African Americans also utilized more direct action in addressing the evils of slavery. Free Black communities developed and implemented ways of protecting and assisting runaway slaves. Free African Americans, especially those in urban settings, began to hide, protect, purchase and sometimes forcibly liberate fugitive slaves. Operating out of the homes and shops of activist African Americans and 'white' people, African Americans formed vigilance committees between 1835 and1846 in New York, Philadelphia and Boston. These organizations were openly formed for the express purpose of "...shelter[ing], defend[ing], and facilitat[ing] the movement of fugitive slaves."[68] In some instances, vigilance committee members physically rescued captured fugitives: "In 1836 a number of Boston's black residents forcibly liberated fugitives Eliza Small and Polly Ann Bates..."[69]

In addition to participation in the Abolitionist movement and the formation of vigilance committees free African Americans participated in symbolic methods of declaring allegiance to the eradication of slavery and support for their fellow African Americans kept in horrible, perpetual bondage. In many northern cities free African Americans celebrated the date of the final elimination of slavery in their individual states as 'Independence Day,' rather than the Fourth of July. Free African Americans also observed the anniversary of Haitian Independence and/or the emancipation of all slaves in the British West Indies.[70] Some free African Americans were able to find the courage, strength of will and commitment, at great personal risk, to lead the charge in eradicating the most pernicious and dangerous impediment to the advancement of all nineteenth century African Americans—slavery, thus, adding yet another filament to the web of the nineteenth century Black community.

~ *Free African American Women in Antebellum America* ~

...as meanly as she is thought of, hindered as she is in all directions, she is always doing something of merit and credit that is not expected of her. She is irrepressible. She is insulted, but she holds up her head; she is scorned, but she proudly demands respect. Thus it has come to pass that the most interesting girl of this country is the colored girl.

—Fannie Barrier Williams, *The Colored Girl*

While the enslaved woman's condition and experience modified the evolution of Black feminist consciousness, discourse, and intellectual enterprise, so too did the condition and experience of *free* Black women in the antebellum south and north. Although these women were free, most had either personally experienced slavery and/or were descendents of enslaved African Americans.[71] In the south free(d) African American women were in a complex position. Black, female, and free in a slaveholding society, these women "...finding themselves neither enslaved nor wholly free, recognized that they were anomalous to the social, economic, [and] legal realities of the Slaveocracy. They were a group apart from both enslaved African Americans and free whites."[72] Most free Black women of the south were urban dwellers, where a coherent Black urban community provided support and protection (i.e. churches and benevolent societies). Such support and protection was generally not available to free Black women living in the rural south, with the exception of the free Black communities established in the lower southern region of the United States.

Free African Americans who lived in the lower South (Alabama, Georgia, Louisiana, Mississippi, and South Carolina) often formed tight-knit communities in small towns or adjoining farms.[73] In such communities Black women formed networks among themselves similar to those of enslaved women. Unlike enslaved women, however, unmarried free Black women had the ability to own property and lay claim to the fruits of their labor. They worked hard to accumulate property and a few were good business women (i.e. independent farmers). But these women mainly performed work that was an extension of the 'domestic sphere' (i.e. domestic servants). Homeownership offered a further opportunity for economic security. Free Black women in the antebellum south could, and did, center their work within their households by taking in boarders, laundry, and sewing. Furthermore, because the legal status of a child always followed that of the *mother*, free Black mothers were able to protect their children from the most dev-astating consequences of slavery—though not from the consequences of racism.

Free Black women's experience, in antebellum America, can be divided into two loose categories: survival and transcendence. The components of these cate-gories, however, were often similar though they operated differently within these two categories. Like their male counterparts, free Black women joined the Black migration north, not only to escape restrictive and oppressive 'Black Laws' but also to embark on a quest for acquisition of their own slice of the 'American Dream'. In fact, free Black women constituted 52% of the antebellum free Black population. "Their numerical superiority was not reflected in their social eco-nomic position, however."[74]

While Black men were nearly completely excluded from obtaining lucrative employment opportunities, Black women had even less opportunity to secure lucrative employment opportunities. For, whether they desired it or not, the larger society had deemed, and were able to enforce, the fact that their Blackness and their *sex* were the central considerations in Black women's lives. Thus, not only were free Black women overwhelmingly unable to acquire a comfortable lif-estyle—for themselves or their children—independently of men, even with the financial contribution of a husband (and/or other male family members) the majority of free Black women were required to either contribute to their families income or, as was more often the case, assume full financial responsibility for themselves and their families. Indeed, the majority of Black women were the 'heads of their households', in fact if not in name. The combined realities of the lack of educational and employment opportunities, coupled with the fact that Black women were essential contributors to the economic survival of their fami-lies, forced Black women to improvise methods to ensure survival. They accom-plished this no small feat in three ways: subsistence labor, household manufacture, and 'outside'/entrepreneurial employment.[75] Black women were adept at finding ways to increase their household provisions *without spending cash* the primary method being scavenging (i.e. for discarded clothing, household wares, and fuel). "…[they] provided the bulk of labor necessary to transform raw materials into items that the family could consume."[76]

Among more prosperous households home and garden manufacture also greatly contributed to a family's survival. Some women home manufactured "…their own candles and their own soap…mattresses, pillows, linens, curtains, and clothing, and repaired furniture and garments."[77] Free Black women in the north could and did center their "outside" work within their households by tak-ing in boarders, laundry, and sewing. In addition, Black women took regular outside work as domestic servants (i.e. cooks, nurses, washerwomen, dressmakers and maids). Still others worked as street vendors "...from sidewalks and carts they hawked roots and herbs they had dug themselves, or fruits, vegetables, candy, eggs, peanuts, coffee, or chocolate."[78]

A number of these women used their profits, from dressmaking, laundering, baking and vending, in innovative entrepreneurial ways: establishing dress-shops, boarding houses, inns, taverns, restaurants, laundering and catering services. Juliet Walker makes a compelling case that antebellum Black businesswomen were indeed entrepreneurs. Walker contends that these women fell within the broad context of the term "...an individual with the ability to make unusual amounts of money using commonly available resources...their activities were characterized by ingenuity, creativity, and innovativeness...[and] a formidable business acumen."[79] Free Black women business entrepreneurs, unfortunately, represented a miniscule minority of free Black women's experience in antebellum America.

While Black women struggled to free themselves from the devastating consequences of racial and gender discrimination, class distinctions were, nevertheless, evident. Class distinctions can be delineated as those of the elite middle-class, the working middle-class, and the poor. Those of the elite middle-class were characterized as possessing extensive informal and/or formal education, and were home and property owners who came from affluent families and married affluent men. Those of the elite middle-class lived "...in ease, comfort and the enjoyment of all the social blessings."[80] Those of the working middle-class were characterized as possessing a limited informal education, may have owned their own homes and/ or other property, and their primary method of participation in the economic aspect of the survival of their families consisted of subsistence labor, home and garden manufacture, and outside employment. Furthermore, a small number of these women were moderately successful as business women and entrepreneurs; "...claiming neither poverty nor riches, yet maintaining, by their pursuits, their families in comparative ease and comfort."[81]

Those of the 'poor class' were characterized as possessing little or no education, did not own their own homes, or any other type of property, and their primary method of participation in the economic aspect of the survival of their families consisted of subsistence labor and outside employment. Most of these women worked their entire lives—as domestics, washerwomen, nannies, and day laborers—from pre-adolescence to their senior years. Tragically, after a lifetime of drudgery, few ever achieved financial security. Moreover, the uncertainties and dangers of life for free African Americans living in the north did not exempt the working middle class or even the elite middle class from "…the ragged edge of solvency."[82] While Black women of the 'higher classes' were able to avoid the most menial and unpleasant jobs usually available to Black women, "…so called middle class females, married and single, were very much working women. Their efforts helped sustain their households."[83] Inevitably, given the fact that the over-whelming majority of free Black women were the heads of their households, or substantial contributors, poverty and lack of educational and economic opportunity had a devastating social impact on the free African American community. "…it is no small wonder that many free women of color became involved in efforts to expand the rights of Black Americans."[84]

As I stated earlier, the uniqueness of Black woman's experience is that she is positioned at the nexus of two of the most well developed ideologies in America: being woman and being Black. The sociocultural trope of Blackness was an essential factor in how the larger society viewed Black women. Moreover, the larger society's sociocultural trope of sex was an essential factor in how *Black men viewed Black women, and how Black women viewed themselves.* "In general, black men emulated the attitudes of their white counterparts towards issues of leadership and gender. The public arena "…was masculine by law, religion, and custom".[85] Amazingly, Black men engaged in the struggle for Black freedom and full access to citizenship rights did not, *chose not*, to see the obvious relationship between the 'special' attention and treatment meted out to Black women, free and enslaved, their own oppression, and the struggle for social and political equality. Free and enslaved women could and did perform menial and skilled jobs equally as laborious as those performed by men. Nevertheless, Black men, in general, seemed unable to grasp the basic absurdity in claiming the very 'manhood rights' that stemmed from a larger society's claims of immutability, law, religion, and custom used to enslave African Americans and oppress free African Americans.

Ironically, it was the Black male leadership's allegiance to the larger society's construction of gender ideology, their insistence on excluding women from membership in Black male associations and organizations (or denial of leadership positions and/or effective voice to the women they allowed to join), their failure to address the pressing concerns of Black women, and the devastating reality of antebellum Black life that encouraged the coalescence of a distinct free Black women's community. To be sure, Black women did not abandon service in male led organizations and societies. Many of the first women's societies, in fact, were formed as auxiliaries to men's groups. Additionally, Black women activists were wholly committed to the uplift of the entire Black community, female and male.

For the most part, Black women did not expend their energies trying to integrate the 'male public sphere'. "They chose instead to radicalize, and were themselves radicalized within their own organizations."[86]

In the effort to expand the rights of African Americans, Black women turned their attention to stabilizing and improving the financial position of Black women. As early as 1783, free Black women in the North began to organize and agitate for better lives—for themselves and their families. Black women living in cities such as Boston, New York, and Philadelphia organized benevolent and mutual aid societies. Like their male counterparts, Black women's benevolent societies collected donations from more affluent African Americans and then dispensed aid and funds to assist the poor. However, Black women's benevolent societies concentrated their efforts on the needs of women and children, particularly widows and orphans. Mutual aid societies, likewise, concentrated on organizing the meager resources of Black women (i.e. establishing mutual aid societies for laundresses and domestic servants). Black women's mutual aid societies, in addition, provided services of particular need and importance to workingwomen. They provided financial and moral support, tended the sick, ran orphanages and makeshift maternity wards, provided babysitting services for working mothers and supported community schools and churches. Moreover, these societies not only provided their much needed services to 'strangers' but also to their own families, friends and neighbors. "Well aware that this month's dispenser of aid might be next month's recipient black women's groups did not...assume that those who gave and those who received would come from different social classes."[87]

Black women community activists were not solely concerned with easing the immediate financial plight of the women of their community. They knew that true equality and full access to better opportunity was the only way to obtain a coveted slice of the 'American Dream'. Their efforts, then, could not focus only on survival but had to take the next logical step as well—transcendence. Thus, free Black women, in tandem with their benevolent and mutual aid activities, waged an unrelenting campaign of individual and community advancement through organizations dedicated to self-improvement and intellectual development—literary societies. Philadelphia represents the 'ground zero' of this movement.

During the Slaveocracy, Philadelphia was home to the largest and best educated free Black community in the North. The formation of Philadelphia's first literary society was the result of a suggestion made by an abolitionist lecturer to the African American male and female audience at a Black national convention held in Philadelphia in 1831. Simeon S. Jocelyn urged Black women to gather together for "…'mental feasts' of moral and religious meditation, conversation, reading and speaking, sympathizing over the fate of the unhappy slave [and] improving their minds…"[88] A few weeks later, a group of Black women founded the Female Literary Association and began constructing an institutional framework. At weekly meetings, devoted to the reading and recitation of original work (poetry and prose), members would bring their unsigned work, an officer would read it aloud, and the other members would offer a critique of the work. "In this way views could be expressed, and stylistic and grammatical corrections made, without embarrassment or personal affront."[89] The success of this association encouraged other Black Philadelphian women to form two more such groups. In October 1834, thirty women founded the Female Minervian Association and, in 1836, another group of women formed the Edgeworth Literary Association. Soon thereafter, free Black literary societies were established in Boston and New York.

Adhering to the old adage that knowledge is power, these associations served many purposes. Weekly meetings provided a safe space from within which Black women could discuss and debate issues of the day and refine their writing skills. Free African American women of the working class, who had been unable to obtain a formal education because they had to work to support themselves and their families, afforded them the opportunity to supplement whatever education they had been able to achieve on their own in a supportive atmosphere. Membership for those of the elite class, who had been educated at home (by private tutors) or at one of the city's private Black schools, afforded the opportunity to "…develop leadership abilities, practice framing constitutions and bylaws, and hone their writing skills."[90]

Moreover, the women who participated in these associations believed, and were able to act on the belief, that possession of a good education was an essential womanly quality. Educated Black women wielded great power—and with this power they could "…effect a fundamental moral and social reformation."[91] With an education Black women could not only pass that education on to their children but also to the entire Black community. Black female literary societies also served to show that when African American women "…showed themselves capable of intellectual improvement they helped to refute the argument that no black person can ever be elevated in this country."[92] Finally, while the members of these literary associations focused on education and intellectual development, they also addressed pressing political concerns important to the Black community especially abolitionism.

Slavery, in the eyes of the antebellum free Black community, was understandably viewed as the greatest obstacle to Black economic, political and social advancement. Black women were as equally committed as Black men in the endeavor to fight, hamper and eradicate slavery. Unfortunately, Black women were overwhelmingly excluded from leadership positions and inclusion in policy and strategy decisions. Moreover, these women strongly believed that the question of gender should be an essential component in the abolitionist agenda and strategy for success. Thus, while they often worked in tandem with men's societies, Black women abolitionists formed their own all-female or gender integrated societies and drew upon their own experiences, as women, to implement ingenious modes of antislavery protest.

Black women abolitionists, for example, drew upon their extensive experience as contributors to the economic survival of their families to develop and implement a boycott of slave produced goods. In 1831 a group of Black women formed the Colored Females Free Produce Society of Philadelphia. The goal of this society was to "…overthrow the economic power of slavery, one bolt of cotton and one teaspoon of sugar at a time."[93] They opened a store stocked only with foods grown and harvested by free farmers; and sold clothes made from 'free materials' and sewn by free hands. The society hosted fairs and picnics, providing access to nonslave merchants. Through newspaper articles and advertisements, they encouraged Americans, Black and white, to boycott slave produced cotton, coffee, rice, sugar, molasses and tobacco in order to "…break the stranglehold of slavery-based economics on the market of the free states."[94] While the Colored Females Free Produce Society of Philadelphia did not measurably cripple the economic empire that was the Slaveocracy, they did accomplish an important part of their overall goal. By drawing a clear line between the direct and indirect economic support that Americans living in the north gave to slavery, they raised the consciousness of both the Black and white communities.

Yet for all their invaluable service to their community and their heroic efforts to ensure the survival of their families, and themselves, antebellum free Black women in the north faced an even greater obstacle in transcending the nineteenth century ideal of feminine respectability. The sociocultural ideal of feminine respectability declared that women were naturally gentle, submissive, weaker than men (physically and mentally), and that they must always take a secondary role in family and community life. Black men, for the most part, accepted this credo and expected Black women to adhere to it. Newspaper articles, sermons from the pulpit, and pronouncements and practices of male led organizations served as the conduits to the Black community for these prescriptive attitudes. For Black women, however, ideals of feminine respectability struck a dissident resonance.

Free Black women tread upon a thin, precarious line that had immense psychological, spiritual and physical ramifications. Just as freedom for African Americans did not confer the full rights and protection of citizenship, freedom, too, did not confer to Black women the rights and protection of feminine respectability. "…free black women were uniformly slandered [by the larger society] as 'degraded' (that is, sexually promiscuous) because of their race."[95] Free Black women were, at all times, painfully aware that this perception, held by the larger society, left them dangerously exposed to sexual violence and rape. In the effort to counteract negative, degrading and dangerous stereotypes of their womanhood, Black women activists in particular focused on propriety and public appearance. They paid careful attention to how they dressed, how they spoke, and how they behaved. They believed that painstaking adherence to this self-imposed regimen of 'lady-like' behavior would not only challenge the slanders heaped upon their womanhood but would prove their respectability. Moreover, the Black male leadership fully expected and encouraged Black women to "…exert all their power to disabuse the public mind of the misrepresentations made of our character."[96]

While Black women had to negotiate their way through the minefield of white hostility, they had an equally complicated relationship with Black men. Black men may have claimed 'manhood rights' in theory but reality was not in par with theory. Reality for the antebellum free Black community was that Black women's economic contribution was an essential component in Black families' survival. And while Black women "…believed it necessary to bolster black men's claims to social power whenever possible" the reality was that Black men *could not* claim the role as family patriarch and sole provider (essential components in antebellum gender convention).[97] Moreover, Black women, on a daily basis, proved their physical and mental strength. They could not, and in some cases *refused* to, don the cloak of the weak, intellectually inferior, and submissive woman. It would soon become glaringly apparent to activist Black women that no matter how hard they tried they would never be able to fully conform to the larger society's or Black men's expectations of feminine respectability. Instead, they would have to construct their own ideal of feminine respectability and in the process they would create "…a community of women who shared a common sense of sociopolitical and cultural identity and who had a moral, civic, and intellectual agenda…"[98]

Black Victorian Feminists and the Black Woman's Era: Identity Re-claimation and Re-formation

In action and attitude…[they] did not hesitate to lay aside their cloaks of decorum and social graces, flex the muscles of their displeasure, and then calmly wrap themselves again in dignity.

—Frances Smith Foster, *A Brighter Coming Day*

On January 1, 1863, President Abraham Lincoln issued the Emancipation Proclamation, and in so doing sounded the final death knoll of the Slaveocracy. Thirty years later, however, African American women were still facing the same battle: "…the fundamental tension between Black women and the rest of society—white men, white women, and to a lesser degree Black men—involved a multifaceted struggle to determine who would control their sexuality…At stake [for Black women]…was the acquisition of personal autonomy and economic liberation." [99] The difference, however, was that Black women were fighting from a new stance freedom—and the mindset such a circumstance engenders. While only a small number of African American women were in a position (socially and financially) to publicly 'agitate' for change, these few initiated an emergent Black feminist discourse and intellectual enterprise. Yet they did so from an extremely unique, complex, and even contradictory vantage point.

While Reconstruction heralded the constitutional conferment of the right of citizenship to all African Americans, and voting rights to Black *men*, post-Reconstruction marked the beginning of the next phase of oppression for African Americans. Buttressed by segregation and disenfranchisement, the triad of race, gender and class oppression threatened the advancement of the post-Slaveocratic Black community. Through defacto and dejure means, the larger community sought to isolate African Americans from, and subjugate them to, the larger American society. "Jim Crow, as segregation was called, quickly pervaded every part of life [of African Americans]…In employment, housing, places of amusement, public transportation, schools, hospitals, and cemeteries, segregation daily produced and reproduced racial identities, power, and disempowerment." [100] Attendant to this 'segregationist movement' was the systematic disenfranchisement of African Americans. "Disenfranchisement, formed part of the larger process of "depoliticalization": literacy tests, poll taxes, and other state election laws, along with social and psychological sanctions such as economic reprisal, violence and threats of violence, effected the mass removal of blacks from the nation's political life. Political institutions and representative government became simply inaccessible and unaccountable to American citizens who happened to be black."[101] In the face of such pervasive and hostile conditions it was clear that the African American community would have to devise and implement its own strategies of social, cultural, and political advancement.

In order to achieve this end, Black intellectuals and community activists developed a concept of racial solidarity defined by a distinct cultural heritage, social relations, and Black institutions. They promoted an ideal of community that encompassed "...the South and the nation, black men and women of different ages and classes, and personally unknown to one another, [this community] perceived and sought to realize a common destiny distinct from that of whites."[102] Black intellectuals and community activists were members of a 'Black movement' that sought to invoke and foster a doctrine of Black pride, self-determination, self-help, economic solidarity, academic achievement, and other forms of individual and collective Black action. Furthermore, their advocacy of a distinct and *cohesive* Black community "...constituted not an escape from the larger American society but an 'alternative structure,' a functional tradition created for the purpose of publicizing black aspirations, giving them political force, and institutionalizing them in forms that might ultimately transform American civilization."[103] This Black intellectual activist movement was the wellspring from which nineteenth century Black Victorian feminists emerged.

One of the most damaging legacies of the Slaveocracy was that of its dehumanization and *defeminization* of Black women. Two tools of implementation, in particular, did the most damage: three hundred plus years of sexual, physical and psychological abuse and persistent degrading images and stereotypes of Black womanhood and sexuality. Sexual exploitation, rape in particular "...has always involved patriarchal notions of women being, at best, not entirely unwilling accomplices, if not outwardly inviting sexual attack."[104] The ideological underpinnings of nineteenth century demeaning and controlling images of Black womanhood was based in the conflation of illicit sexuality, promiscuity, and Black womanhood. Yet there is another prevalent theme of their experience—enslaved women's endeavor to resist sexual exploitation and the reclamation of their bodies and sexual selves. Enslaved women fashioned positive, even heroic, self-images. These images depicted enslaved women as self-reliant, self-determined survivalists. Thus, a history and continuing threat of sexual exploitation critically informed the evolution of Black feminist ideology and activism. "[What were]...the consequences of child abuse and sexual abuse on an entire society in which beating and raping of enslaved people was neither secret nor metaphorical

[?]."[105] One consequence was Black women's development of a '*culture of dissemblance*'—or the erection of a veil of secrecy to shield the truth of their inner lives from the larger (white) society. The 'culture of dissemblance' was an integral part of the enslaved woman's community and, by necessity, this method of self-imposed invisibility extended into the nineteenth century Black woman's community and culture. Within this culture Black women created a 'space,' a haven, from which to individually and collectively create positive and powerful self-images; counterimages to the larger culture's demeaning images of Black womanhood. Undoubtedly, the construction and maintenance of a 'culture of dissemblance' also assisted Black women to effectively function while "...all the while living within a clearly hostile white, patriarchal, middle-class America."[106]

Adoption of this self-imposed invisibility, however, unwittingly contributed to impeding of Black women's realization of the attainment of respect, control over their own sexuality, and better access to educational and economic opportunity. In other words, controlling/demeaning stereotypes of Black womanhood filled the space left empty of representations of the realities of African American women's lives. Someone had to willingly abdicate self-imposed invisibility in order to disseminate alternate images of Black womanhood for public viewing. Only a few women were willing and able to act, boldly and courageously, and attempt to alter the position of all African American women in American society. I call these women—who *chose* to step from behind the veil—*Black Victorian Feminists.*

There are two terms that are complex and, at the outset, seemingly contradictory that I will apply to this group of women that are of particular importance in this dissertation—*Victorian* and *feminist.* I apply the term *Victorian* to these women because Victorian ideals and lifestyle were the bedrock they adhered to and advocated for the Black community. Beginning during the Slaveocracy, American gender and race ideologies combined to create a complicated set of myths about Black and white womanhood. The effect was to place white women upon a pedestal while simultaneously placing Black women beneath said pedestal. "The attributes of True Womanhood, by which a woman judged herself and was judged by her husband, her neighbors, and society could be divided into four cardinal virtues—piety, purity, submissiveness, and domesticity. Put them together and they spelled mother, daughter, sister, wife—woman. Without them no matter whether there was fame, achievement or wealth, all was ashes. With them she was promised happiness and power."[107]

The tenets of this 'cult of true womanhood' formed the dominant socio-ideological model that governed societal opinions about women's behavior and women's status. True women were Ladies. The trope of 'Lady' represented a differentiated, elite, status within the overarching conception of woman. The 'cult of true womanhood' set the parameters under which a woman was deemed to be eligible or ineligible to adopt the title of 'Lady;' within this socio-ideological model "…no black woman, regardless of income, education, refinement or character enjoyed the status of lady." [108] By the late nineteenth century, the social conceptions of white womanhood may have fluctuated but one thing remained constant: the denial of the inclusion of African American women into the ranks of true womanhood.

Of paramount importance to Black Victorian feminist's re-formative efforts were the refutation and dismantling of the negative stereotypes of Black womanhood that prevailed in the nineteenth century American psyche, and/or inclusion into the ranks of true womanhood. In order to achieve this end, Black Victorian feminists appropriated white Victorian middle class ideals of 'traditional' gender roles and views on sexuality as an essential element in their re-clamation of Black womanhood. Black Victorian feminists "…felt compelled to downplay, even deny, sexual expression"[109] and adhered to and promoted an ideology of respectability that linked public behavior and individual self-respect to the elevation of Black womanhood and the advancement of the Black community. "They felt certain that 'respectable' behavior in public would earn their people a measure of esteem from white America, and hence they strove to win the black lower class's psychological allegiance to temperance, industriousness, thrift, refined manners, and Victorian sexual morals."[110]

Middle class status, too, was an important factor in Black Victorian feminist ideology. By the late nineteenth century, thirty years of 'freedom', northern migration, urbanization, and increasing education and economic opportunity contributed to the development of the Black middle class. "A major force in the expansion of the Black middle class…was the rise in number and importance of educated, professional (and, sometimes, financially successful) Black women."[111] Black middle class women can be categorized as belonging to three overlapping groups: the Upper Middle Class Social Elite, the New Professional Middle Class, and the Lower Middle Class.

For the women of the Upper Middle Class Social Elite, their status was a birthright conferred by the educational, financial, and professional success of their families. "These women were frequently touted as the most representative of Black womanhood, partly to combat widespread racist theories about Black female immorality and lack of respectability."[112] The New Professional Middle Class, however, comprised the largest group of the Black middle class. Their status was not a birthright but was conferred by their personal academic, financial, and professional success. Often raised in poverty, the majority of this group had either been enslaved themselves or were the daughters of 'slaves'. An important characteristic of the New Professional Middle Class was the belief that bloodlines, income, occupation, and/or education did not automatically render an individual eligible or ineligible of possessing moral character, refinement, respectability, or the potential to attain an elevated womanhood. Imbued with "…the cultural values of ordinary Black folk…they were personally aware of the abilities and strengths of hardworking, church-going ordinary Black folk."[113] The Lower Middle Class was comprised of women who were domestic workers, street vendors, business owners, and those who participated in a host of entrepreneurial enterprises. While the majority of their income was used to ensure the economic survival of their families, Black women of the Lower Middle Class were also active in their communities; they donated their time and nickels and dimes in order to support their local schools, churches, and a myriad of Black organizations and institutions. Yet, whether a member of the Social Elite, the New Professional, or the Lower Middle Class, Black middle class women were aware that they were ultimately dependent upon the recognition and allegiance of the 'Black masses'. "For legitimation as a leadership class…[Black Victorian feminists] understood their individual status and well-being in American society [rested] ultimately with the status and well-being of the larger black population."[114]

I deliberately apply the contemporary term *feminist* to these nineteenth century women in order to emphasize and better conceptualize the fact that Black Victorian Feminist ideology and activism was rooted in an identity re-claimation and re-formation that was both *radical* and *libratory*. It is important to remember, however, that these women did not necessarily define *themselves* as feminists (with the possible exception of Ida B. Wells (Barnett) and may have rejected the term all-together. This group of women, for the most part, did not question traditional culturally prescribed roles for women—they had a *different understanding* of these roles. The fact that they did speak about the moral integrity of Black women, lynching, poverty, institutionalized racism and sexism, the racism of white women and men, the sexism of Black men, lobbied for the vote and access to educational and economic opportunity attests to the fact that while these women may not have viewed themselves as, and may have rejected the label, feminist, they could and did write and act in a feminist vein.

This small cadre of women boldly stepped forward to fill the 'public space' left empty of true representations of Black women's lives with their hitherto private positive and empowering self-images. And, in the process, they strove not only for the elevation of Black womanhood but for the advancement of their 'race' as well. Black Victorian Feminists re-constructed the trope of race from one of Black oppression to one of Black liberation. "[They] took 'race' and empowered its language with their own meaning and intent…race signified a cultural identity that defined and connected blacks as a people, even as a nation…[Black Victorian Feminists] fashioned race into a cultural identity that resisted white hegemonic discourses."[115] The goal was to negate negative white stereotypes of African Americans and supplant them with a Black worldview and/or standpoint. They were 'romantic racialists' who justified and valorized the Black community as contributors of their own 'special gifts' to humanity. I utilize the term feminist in order to underscore the fact that Black Victorian Feminists created a distinct ideology and implemented a distinct methodology in order to bring about a radical change in their circumstance. Finally, the term feminist is essential to this discussion because it denotes the fact that Black Victorian Feminist ideology and methodology was rooted in Black culture and the subversion of the triad of oppression.

Through their appropriation and subversion of the tenets of the 'cult of true womanhood', Black Victorian feminists sought to refute and dismantle the demeaning and degrading stereotypes of Black womanhood. The trope of class served as another one of the prongs of the triad of oppression. As with the ideology of true womanhood, Black Victorian feminists subverted the dominant conception of class and re-created one that reflected their particular viewpoint, circumstance, and goal. Within the larger community, 'race' was one of the designations of class; a designation that did not include African Americans: "The actual class positions of blacks did not matter, nor did the acknowledgement of differential statuses (such as by income, type of employment, morals and manners, education, or color) by blacks themselves. An entire system of cultural preconceptions disregarded these complexities and tensions by grouping all blacks into a normative well of inferiority and subserviency."[116] For Black Victorian feminists, then, claiming the right of inclusion of African Americans into the ranks of the bourgeoisie was a resistant and libratory endeavor—providing another battleground from which Black women could agitate for the elevation of Black womanhood and the uplift of the entire African American community.

3

REVOLUTIONARY PETUNIAS

Be nobody's darling; Be an outcast. Take the contradictions of your life. And wrap around you like a shawl, to parry stones, to keep you warm.

—Alice Walker, *Revolutionary Petunias*

African American women had been working for the 'elevation of the race' since the dark days of the Slaveocracy. The self-defined/self-valued development of Black womanhood had been ongoing for decades (if not centuries) behind the veil of a culture of dissemblance. Nonetheless, by the late nineteenth century, Black Victorian Feminists were continually confronted with the fact that social status, academic achievement, and economic prosperity did not exempt them, or the larger Black community, from the humiliations of oppression. Despite their relative privilege and accomplishments, Black Victorian Feminists, and all Black women, continued to be linked to illicit sexuality and were denied the right to control their sexuality, acquire personal autonomy and enjoy unfettered access to economic opportunity. A small cadre of women bravely shed their protective cloak and began to publicly agitate for change. The World's Congress of Representative Women unwittingly provided the ideal platform from which the entire world would witness an emergent discourse and intellectual enterprise that was proudly Black and feminist to its core.

Hallie Quinn Brown, Anna Julia Cooper, Fanny Jackson Coppin, Sarah Jane Early, Frances Ellen Watkins Harper, Ida Bell Wells and Fannie Barrier Williams comprised the unofficial delegation of Black Victorian Feminists intent on introducing to America, and the world, the future of Black womanhood,: "American literature, American art, and American music will be enriched by production having new and peculiar features of interest and excellence...The exceptional career of our women will yet stamp itself indelibly upon the thought of this country."

An overview of the life experiences of this delegation is needed in order to fully examine the historical implications of their involvement at the World's Columbian Exposition. Moreover, such an examination will further establish their participation in the creation of an emergent Black feminist discourse and intellectual enterprise.

Sarah Jane Woodson Early was born 15 November 1825 in Chillicothe, Ohio to Thomas and Jemimma (Riddle) Woodson. Thomas was the son of Thomas Jefferson and Sally Hemmings "...the slave girl who was the half sister to Jefferson's dead wife."[117] Thomas Woodson was able to purchase his own and his family's freedom for $900.00. Upon obtaining freedom, he moved his family from Greenbriar County, Virginia to Chillicothe, Ohio in 1820. The Woodson family immediately joined the local Methodist Church. They and the other Black families in the church, however, strongly objected to the discriminatory treatment they experienced in the church. They were "...seated separately...apart from white members and...[were] given communion after the whites."[118] The Woodsons and the other Black families decided to leave that church and organize their own Black Methodist Church. In 1830 the Woodsons and the Black community went one step further and established an all Black farming community in Berlin Crossroads, Milton Township, Jackson County, Ohio—thereby severing ties with the oppressive white community. Ten years after its founding, the Berlin Crossroads Black Community consisted of twenty-three families and Thomas Woodson personally owned four hundred acres of land, making him worth several thousand dollars in real estate.[119] Early's parents provided her with the rare and incredibly empowering childhood experience of being raised in a community of "self-sufficient black farmers owning their own land, harvesting their own crops, helping each other build their homes, worshipping in their own church and supporting their own school."[120] Moreover, Early's parents and brothers were educated community builders who encouraged their youngest child, and sibling, to do and be the same. In 1852 Early enrolled at Oberlin College.

In 1835, the trustees of the Oberlin Collegiate Institute declared, "the education of people of color is a matter of great interest and should be encouraged and sustained at this institution."[121] With this declaration, Oberlin College became the only college in America open to Black women (until after the Civil War) and thus it profoundly impacted the educational goals and achievements of Black women. Oberlin offered three courses: the Preparatory Department (especially important to Black women who had received an inadequate secondary education); the Young Ladies Course (LC) "...comparable to the curriculum at women's seminaries;" and the College course, also known as the 'gentleman's course' (the equivalent of a baccalaureate degree).[122] The Oberlin faculty, staff, and white student body were committed to creating and maintaining a safe, welcoming environment for their Black student body and it seems as though the Black student body got the message experiencing Oberlin as an "interracial utopia, recalling that they had been members and officers of the literary society, and had roomed and eaten along with their white classmates in college dormitories and dining halls."[123] Naturally, Oberlin College attracted Black women from across the nation seeking educational opportunity in a safe and welcoming environment. Thirteen years later another institution of higher learning would become an essential factor in the cultivation of these seven women's lives and the evolution of Black Victorian Feminism.

In 1847 Elder Daniel A. Payne founded Wilberforce University (originally named Union Seminary). Payne's goal was to provide the "…instruction of the youth of Negro people in various branches of literature, science, agriculture, and mechanical arts."[124] Wilberforce University was the first of its kind: and institution of higher learning founded by African Americans for African Americans. As such, a unique community was born and evolved around this school. The Wilberforce community was diverse and fluid, characterizing and accommodating the unique antebellum free Black community. "The result was a community with a relatively high standard of living, where a considerable premium was placed on learning and the arts."[125] Such a community, quite understandably, attracted African Americans from across the nation, seeking education and economic opportunity in a safe and welcoming environment.

In 1852, Early began the 'Gentleman's Course' at Oberlin College. She worked her way through college by teaching, during school breaks, at schools in Circleville and Portsmouth, Ohio. After graduating from Oberlin in 1856, Early spent the next ten years teaching at Black schools in Chillicothe, Gallipolis, Zanesville, Hillsboro, and Hamilton. In 1858, she was appointed 'Preceptress of English and Latin and Lady Principal and Matron at Wilberforce University, becoming the first African American member of a college faculty. After ten years in that position, Early left her position and accepted a position with the Freedman's Bureau[126], teaching at a girl's school in Hillsboro, North Carolina. Later that year, at the age of 43, she married Jordan Winston Early[127]. During her marriage, Early continued to teach in black schools, in Tennessee, wherever her husband's churches were located[128]. By the time she retired in 1888, Sarah Jane Early had "…taught over 6,000 children, and served as a school principal in segregated schools in four major cities."[129]

For Early, moral reform was an essential component in the effort to 'uplift the race' and elevate Black womanhood. Early described the Black church as "an open door by which to enter the arena of public action. Long had she waited for moral and intellectual recognition from the world. Too long had the veil of obscurity, like the gall of death, shut out the knowledge of her existence from the sisterhood of earth."[130] Before her appearance at the Exposition, Early was wholly dedicated to her chosen arena of activism: the Black Church and the Temperance Movement. Temperance (abstinence from drinking alcohol) was touted, by the church, to be one of the necessary ingredients of the Black uplift ethic. Black Victorian Feminists also linked sobriety to the attributes of womanhood and the elevation of Black womanhood. "No woman can accomplish the greatest functions of her sex, replenishing the earth and rearing her children in an atmosphere of sweet purity—with a body weakened by the ravages of alcohol—or a mind made torpid by drink…Let us then be sober."[131]

A dedicated and eloquent leader of the cause, Early served as Superintendent of the Colored Division of the Woman's Christian Temperance Union from 1888 to 1892. In 1890 the National Temperance Missionary Society offered her a lecture position; she accepted and for the next four years she traveled and lectured in support of the cause. In an annual report to the Women's Christian Temperance Union, Early provides a glimpse of how far reaching and successful her efforts were: "I have conversed with more than three hundred ministers and teachers in five different states and pledged them to work. I have visited two national ecclesiastical conferences…I have visited and spoken to twelve institutions of learning…I have visited and labored in prisons with inmates of five institutions, and I have labored in many Sabbath schools and day schools, or wherever I could find young people or old people assembled."[132] In 1894, Early published a biography about her husband—*The Life and Labors of Reverend Early*. She and her husband lived and worked in his ministry, in Nashville, Tennessee, until his death in 1903. Sarah Jane Early died of heart disease, at her home, 15 August 1907.

Frances Ellen Watkins Harper was born to free parents, 24 September 1825, in the slave city of Baltimore, Maryland. Other than her birth date, the 'status' of her parents, and the fact that Harper was orphaned at the age of three. there are no existing records pertaining to the names and lives of her parents. Harper was reared by, and attended the school of, her uncle William Watkins, "…a fervent abolitionist, a community leader, and a highly regarded teacher."[133] Watkins founded and ran the William Watkins Academy for Negro Youth. The Academy "…was well known for its emphasis upon biblical studies, the classics, and elocution…Greek and Latin were a major part of the curriculum…".[134] The Academy was so well regarded for its superior classical education that, like Wilberforce University, slaveholders from neighboring states sent their biracial children there to be educated. "Harper's intense commitment to abolitionist and other social welfare crusades, her familiarity with classical and Christian mythology, and her reputation for oratory and general deportment were obviously influenced by her education at the academy."[135]

Although Harper's 'formal' education ended when she was thirteen, she was determined to continue her quest for knowledge. Harper procured a position as a domestic and child care provider. Her employers owned a bookstore and allowed her to read from their shelves in her spare time. "While still in adolescence, she acquired a reputation as an intelligent, talented young writer…"[136] writing and publishing articles and poems in various periodicals. In 1845, Harper published her first book of prose entitled *Forest Leaves*. In 1852, local officials forced William Watkins to sell his house and his school and, soon thereafter, Watkins moved his family to Canada, Harper left Maryland too, accepting a teaching position at Union Seminary in Ohio. Two years later she accepted a teaching position in Little York, Pennsylvania.

In 1854 Harper moved to Philadelphia, Pennsylvania where she became heavily involved in the abolitionist movement. Soon thereafter, the Maine Anti-Slavery Society hired Harper as a traveling lecturer, the first Black woman to be so employed. 1854 also marks the year that Harper published *Poems on Miscellaneous Subjects*. Published in both Boston and Philadelphia the work was very successful; so much so that both editions were reprinted in 1855. Between 1857 and 1861 Harper worked the abolitionist circuit as a lecturer for the Pennsylvania Anti-Slavery Society and the Ohio State Anti-Slavery Society, consecutively; worked with Black abolitionists in Michigan, New Jersey, New York, Ohio, and Pennsylvania; and was an agent for the Underground Railroad.

On 22 November 1860, Harper married Fenton Harper and soon thereafter gave birth to a daughter, Mary. While she did limit her appearances thereafter, she continued to publish and lecture. Sadly, Harper was widowed in 1864. Five months after Fenton Harper died, Frances Harper moved with her daughter to New England and promptly resumed her career. Harper supported herself and her daughter through book sales and public speaking engagements. Harper also remained very active within and without the Black community she continued to publish her poems and short stories in journals and periodicals as well as publishing *Moses: A Story of the Nile* (1869); *Poems* (1871); *Sketches of Southern Life* (1872). She served as superintendent of the Philadelphia and Pennsylvania colored chapters of the Women's Christian Temperance Union; and, in 1893 published her most famous work *Iola Leroy, Or, Shadows Uplifted*.

Harper, too, was involved in temperance work. In fact, she also held the position of Superintendent of the Colored Division of the Woman's Christian Temperance Union in the years directly preceding Sarah Jane Early. As part of her temperance work, Harper regularly published articles and essays in the *African Methodist Episcopal Church Review*. Once such article was "The Woman's Christian Temperance Union and the Colored Woman." In it Harper affirms that temperance work provided an arena for many Black Victorian Feminists to find and utilize a 'public voice' and agitate for change. "Lips that had been silent in the prayer meeting were loosened to take part in the wonderful uprising…Among the most notable epochs in this era is the uprising of women against the twin evils of slavery and intemperance, which had foisted themselves like leeches upon the civilization of the present age."[137] In 1896, Harper was elected vice-president of the National Council of Negro Women.

Between 1892 and 1900, Harper published four volumes of poetry and a novel, all the while continuing to travel on the lecture circuit. Unfortunately, there is little in the public record of Harper's life and activities after 1901. Moreover, Harper left no diaries or journals and did not publish and autobiography. However, in an letter to her close friend, Reverend Francis J. Grimke, Harper related her hopes for the future: "…look beyond the present pain with hope for a better and brighter future, in which love shall conquer hate, and both branches of the human family in this country will realize that their interests and duties all like in one direction, and that we cannot violate the one without dissevering the other."[138] At the age of eighty-five, Frances Ellen Watkins Harper died of heart failure in Philadelphia, Pennsylvania, 20 February 1911.

Fanny Jackson Coppin was born a slave in Washington, D.C. (1837). While her enslaved grandfather bought his own and several of his children's' freedom "…on account of my [Coppin's] birth, my grandfather refused to buy my mother; and so I was left a slave…"[139] Coppin's devoted aunt Sarah worked, earning six dollars per month, to buy Coppin's freedom. After saving one hundred and twenty-five dollars Aunt Sarah bought Coppin's freedom and sent her to live with another aunt in New Bedford, Massachusetts. There Coppin was put out to work "…at a place where I was allowed to go to school when not at work."[140] When she was fourteen, Coppin was sent to Newport, Rhode Island to live with, yet another aunt, Elizabeth Orr, but she was reluctant to over tax her aunt's meager resources. So, she found a position as a live-in domestic in the home of George and Elizabeth Calvert. "Here I had one hour every other afternoon in the week to take some private lessons…After that I attended for a few months at the public colored school."[141] It was while Coppin was a student at the Rhode Island State Normal School that she first heard the call to strive for a higher education and become an educator: "…it was in me to get an education and to teach my people. This idea was deep in my soul. Where it came from I cannot tell, for I had never had any exhortations, nor any lecture which influenced me to take this course. It must have been born in me."[142] Thus, with the aid of her Aunt Sarah and a nine-dollar a year scholarship from Bishop Daniel Payne, Coppin was able to pay her way to Oberlin College in 1860.

Every year the faculty at Oberlin chose the best forty students, from the junior and senior classes, to teach the preparatory classes—Coppin was among the chosen in 1863(?), her junior year. She was such a successful and popular teacher that her class was divided into two classes in order to meet the enrollment demand. Besides teaching two preparatory classes and keeping up with her studies, Coppin tutored sixteen students privately and formed a night school (1865) teaching newly emancipated African Americans to read and write: "I felt that for such people to have been kept in the darkness of ignorance was an unpardonable sin…"[143] Coppin's night school was an unadulterated success and her efforts drew acclaim from both the Black and white communities. In 1865, Coppin graduated from Oberlin, the second Black woman to so, and accepted a teaching position at the Institute for Colored Youth in Philadelphia, Pennsylvania, the oldest private high school for African American youth: "Here I was given the delightful task of teaching my own people…"[144].

Richard Humphrey's, a Philadelphia goldsmith, founded the Institute for Colored Youth in Philadelphia in 1832. Humphreys bequeathed ten thousand dollars for the establishment of a school for African Americans; a thirteen-member board of Quakers was established in order to supervise the project. In 1840, the board of trustees purchased a one hundred and thirty-six acre farm, on the outskirts of Philadelphia, and established a farm school for African American boys. "The stringent rules and regulations resulted in a series of runaways and by 1846 the unsuccessful farm school had closed."[145] Two years later, a group of Black Philadelphia tradesmen approached the board and proposed the establishment of an educational institution "…where Black students could be apprenticed with them to learn various trades and also have an opportunity to study the literary and "higher branches"."[146] The board agreed and a night school was opened in South Philadelphia in 1849. The night school was so successful that the tradesmen again approached to board with the proposal to establish a co-educational day school that would offer a classical, college preparatory curriculum—the Institute for Colored Youth; again the board agreed. "In 1852, a building was erected at Sixth and Lombard streets in the heart of the Philadelphia Black community."[147] In 1869 the principal of the Institute left his position in order to accept an appointment as the United States minister of Haiti. Coppin was offered and accepted the position, becoming the first African American woman high school principal in America.

In 1881, Coppin married Levi Coppin, an African Methodist Episcopal minister. Levi approved of and actively supported his wife's decision to continue her career after her marriage. For the first three years of their marriage, Mr. Coppin was pastor of a church in Baltimore, Maryland and commuted to Philadelphia, Pennsylvania where Coppin continued her successful career as principal of the Institute. "Levi Coppin seemed genuinely proud to be married to such a distinguished and well regarded woman. He often spoke of her with deep respect, admiration, and appreciation."[148] In 1884, Mr. Coppin joined his wife in Philadelphia, transferring to a small church. After her marriage, Mrs. Coppin became an active member of the African Methodist Episcopal Church. Coppin was as supportive of her husband's career as he was of hers: "Although Coppin was devoted to the institute, during the summers she often traveled with her husband for the A.M.E. Church."[149] Coppin was elected president of the local Women's Mite Missionary and, soon thereafter, was elected president of the Women's Home and Foreign Missionary Society of the A.M.E. Church; she was a representative for the organization at the Centenary of Missions Conference in London, England in 1888.

Besides brilliantly executing her duties as principal of the Institute, Coppin was active in the Black community. She worked tirelessly "…to find employment and housing for her students and other African Americans in Philadelphia."[150] Furthermore, she successfully lobbied for the establishment of an industrial training department at the Institute. After ten years of fund-raising, Coppin realized her goal when the industrial training department opened in January of 1889. "…the department [offered] training in carpentry, bricklaying, shoemaking, printing, plastering, millinery, dressmaking, and cooking. The department was the first trade school for African Americans in Philadelphia."[151]

By the turn of the century, a lifetime of hard work and achievement had seriously affected Coppin's health. In 1896, she became ill with Pleurisy (inflammation of the lungs) and was bedridden. Coppin never fully recovered and in 1901 her failing health forced her to retire from her beloved Institute for Colored Youth. Refusing to allow her poor health to completely end her career, Coppin continued to serve as a member of the board of managers for the Home for Aged and Infirmed Colored People in Philadelphia (1882–1913). She was also elected as one of the vice-presidents of the National Association of Colored Women. In 1902 Coppin accompanied her husband to Cape Town, South Africa. "[She] devoted her stay to developing missions among the women of the country."[152] Coppin had a profound impact on the women she befriended. The African missions raised $10,000 in order to build the Fanny Jackson Coppin Girls Hall in her honor.

Yet for all the accolades, Coppin believed that her contributions were but a small part in the overall endeavor for the elevation of Black womanhood, at home and abroad: "To go to Africa, the original home of our people…and to contribute, even in a small degree, toward the development, civil and religious, that is going on among them, is a privilege that anyone might be glad to enjoy."[153] The Coppins left Cape Town in 1903, embarked on an extensive tour of Europe, and returned to the United States in the spring of 1904. Soon thereafter, Reverend Coppin was appointed bishop of the Seventh Episcopal District of the African Methodist Episcopal Church. Sadly, by 1905 Coppin's health had so deteriorated the Coppins returned to Philadelphia and for the final eight years of her life, Coppin was primarily homebound. Nevertheless, she found the strength and wherewithal to write and publish *Reminiscences of School Life and Hints on Teaching* in 1913.

Reminiscences consists of four sections. The first is an autobiographical sketch. The second is a comprehensive treatise on the art of teaching and the field of education; addressing such topic as methods for teaching a classical curriculum, morals and good manners. The third section is a travel diary of her experiences and adventures in England and South Africa. The final section consists of biographical sketches of the faculty and students Coppin knew and/or interacted with at the Institute for Colored Youth during her tenure there as a teacher and administrator. Astoundingly, Coppin published *Reminiscences* in the last year of her life. Levi Coppin was one of many who realized that Fanny Jackson Coppin's life was an important component of nineteenth century Black women's experience and voice. In the preface to the book he wrote: "The author of this work was frequently urged by friends to write, and for publication, something that would present a view of the writer's early life, as well as give some of her methods of imparting the intellectual and moral instruction that has proved so eminently successful in influencing and moulding so many lives."[154] On 21 January 1913 Fanny Jackson Coppin died at her home in Philadelphia.

Hallie Quinn Brown was born 10 March 1845 in Pittsburgh, Pennsylvania to educated parents. Her father, Thomas Brown, was a former slave from Frederick

County, Maryland. His Scots grandmother allowed him, to buy his freedom from her on his twenty-fifth birthday (1834). Soon thereafter, he purchased the freedom of his father, his sister Ann, and his brother. Thomas Brown "...was a man of remarkable character and intellect."[155] Known as the 'walking encyclopedia,' Thomas Brown worked as a steward and express agent on the riverboats traveling from Pittsburgh to New Orleans. Hallie Brown's mother, Frances Jane Scroggins, was also born enslaved. Her grandfather, a Virginia planter and Revolutionary War veteran, emancipated Frances, her mother—Ellen Ann, and her three sisters—Harriet, Eliza Anne and Martha Ellen. Emancipation, however, left them homeless and destitute. The situation became so dire that Scroggins and her sisters were 'bound out'. "In what amounted to legal reenslavement, apprenticeship laws allowed whites to keep and employ black children under the age of twenty-one whose parents or relatives were deemed by a court to be either unfit or unable to be kept off the public dole."[156] In later years, Scroggins told her daughter, Hallie, about the harsh treatment she received at the hands of her 'bond mistress': "...lack of food, clothes, and sharp reproof; [and] often stripes from a leather tawse upon her bare shoulders."[157] Sometime during her childhood, Scroggins and her family migrated from the 'slave state' of Virginia to the 'free state' of Ohio. After several years of living in Ohio, Sroggins "...became deeply interested in the cause of the slaves and joined the Abolitionists. She had several narrow escapes from being arrested."[158]

Thomas Brown, then thirty-two years old, and Frances Scroggins, then twenty-two years old, married in 1841 and made their home, first in Salem, Ohio and then on Hazel Street in Pittsburgh, Pennsylvania. Thomas and Frances Brown had six children, Hallie was the fifth. The Browns used their home as a way station for, and were conductors on, the Underground Railroad[159]. "Having seen the horrors of slavery together they espoused the cause of the slave and fought his battle...many a hunted fugitive found food, shelter and encouragement while waiting to be sent to Canada."[160] As activists in the anti-slavery movement, Thomas and Frances Brown consciously exposed their children to the risks and rewards of resistance. Years later Brown recounted "At one time a mother and five children remained one cold winter hidden by Mrs. [Frances] Brown...at another time, a family...escaped from Texas and were cared for in their home for weeks."[161] Thomas Brown often recounted his harrowing yet successful experiences aiding fugitive slaves. At an early age Brown learned of the oppression that slavery represented to African Americans. One of Frances Brown's recollections, in particular, gave a young Hallie Brown a glimpse into the horrors of the Slaveocracy. One morning when Frances Brown was a little girl, her mother sent her to the town pump to draw water. While she was there a man on a horse with a "…long line of naked slaves two by two, chained to each other" stopped at the pump. "…with the crack of the whip, he dashed down the road, the slaves running at full speed to keep pace…For days together, she could not lose sight of those poor creatures with wild staring eyes and tongues lolled out lapping the water like dumb, thirsty animals."[162] By the time that Hallie Brown was old enough to hear and understand these stories, the Brown family was living a comfortable middle class life. Nonetheless, Brown was deeply affected by the tales her mother and father told.

Besides his work as a steward and express agent on the riverboats, and activities with the Abolitionist movement and the Underground Railroad, Thomas Brown was an active congregant at the local African Methodist Episcopal church "…traveling through the states of Pennsylvania, Ohio, and Kentucky collecting funds to build the Old Wylie Avenue A.M.E. Church…"[163] Besides her work with the Abolitionist movement and the Underground Railroad, Frances Brown raised a family and worked alongside her husband in the church "…with women of the church [she] raised great funds at home."[164] The Brown family home did not only serve as a way station for fugitive slaves, visiting prominent Black community leaders, too, often stayed: "Their home became a haven of rest for the weary, travelling minister…From this home, while the A.M.E. General Conference was in session in Pittsburgh, Daniel A. Payne was elected Bishop."[165] Thus Brown, was not only raised in an 'abolitionist household,' she was gifted with continued exposure to and interaction with educated and intelligent Black men and women who were community leaders and community builders. Although the Browns were active in the Black community and had achieved economic prosperity, "Their greatest ambition was to give their children useful education."[166] The eldest children: Jere, Belle, Anne and Mary, were students at Avery College. In 1864, due to Mrs. Brown's poor health, the family moved to Chatham, Ontario and bought a farm, on the Ninth Concession, County of Kent. Eventually, Mrs. Brown's health improved and the family elected to return to the United States in 1870. By this time the eldest of the Brown children had their own families; only Hallie and her younger brother John remained at home.

Another equally important influence in Brown's life, that would have life long effects, began when Thomas and Frances Brown moved their two remaining children to Wilberforce, Ohio—for the sole purpose of procuring an excellent education for their two youngest children. Once there Hallie and John Brown enrolled at Wilberforce University. Hallie Quinn Brown graduated from Wilberforce University with a baccalaureate degree in 1873. Like her parents before her,

Brown immediately began a lifelong endeavor to 'uplift' the Black community and elevate Black womanhood—she became a teacher.

Brown's first teaching position was in South Carolina; there she taught Black children and adults, from various plantations, how to read and write. Soon thereafter, she supervised a school on the Sonora plantation, in Mississippi, and held teaching positions in the city public schools of Yazoo, Mississippi and Columbia, South Carolina. From 1875–1879, Brown taught in the Dayton, Ohio public school system. She served as dean of Allen University at Columbia, Ohio and, simultaneously, ran a night school for adults, (1885–1887). Moreover, Brown studied at the Chautauqua Lecture School, graduating as salutatorian of her class in 1886. She served as dean of women at Tuskegee Institute (1887–1888); and in 1890 she was awarded an honorary M.S. degree from Wilberforce University. In 1893, Brown was appointed professor of elocution at Wilberforce University, where she spent the rest of her educational career.

Hallie Quinn Brown's exposure to and interaction with Black women of the abolitionist movement, women who were educated, intelligent community leaders and builders, with fugitive slave women brave and desperate enough to take their destinies into their own hands, and the women of the Wilberforce community nourished in her an unshakable belief in the existence and redemptive power of Black womanhood. Moreover her greatest example, according to Brown, was that of her mother—Frances Brown. In her remembrances of her mother Brown, in a manner unique to Black Victorian Feminists, painted a picture of Black womanhood that appropriates white Victorian gender convention and subverts them at the same time. Brown described her mother as "…the guiding star of the home [who] ruled her household by love and gentleness."[167] Brown was clearly referring to the tenets of the cult of true womanhood.

She went on, however, to state that when her father was arrested during the Civil War and imprisoned for nearly one year, her mother quickly went about the business of protecting and caring for herself and her six children: "Not knowing how long he would be detained, she began with that calm, quiet spirit, full of determination and action…to plan for the comfort of her family."[168] Similarly, once the family settled in Wilberforce, Mrs. Brown continued to be an advocate for the local Black community, centering her activism on Wilberforce University students: "She befriended scores of poor, worthy students and for thirty years brought into her home young men and women to work for their board but treated [them] as members of the family."[169] Mrs. Brown also continued to be an active member of the Black church and was "…one of the first members of the College Aid Society, an organization founded to assist indigent students."[170] Following the example set by scores of Black women, her mother in particular Brown defined a true woman as one who not only took care of her family and her home, but also ensured that her daughters received as extensive an education as her sons, aided and abetted fugitive slaves and was a community leader and builder.

In 1893, based on her training in articulation, enunciation, and pronunciation, Brown was appointed professor of Elocution at Wilberforce University. In nineteenth century America and Europe, elocution was admired and respected as a discipline. Brown's skill at elocution and public speaking served as the foundation of her career and provided many opportunities. She was a member of the Wilberforce Concert Company "…a group which traveled Europe to promote a better international view of the American black…and gave 'pieces' before King George V and Queen Mary of Great Britain."[171] While in London, Brown addressed the Third Biennial Convention of the World's Woman's Christian Temperance Union and was a representative to the International Congress of Women. After returning to the United States, Brown returned to her duties at Wilberforce University.

In 1910, Brown returned to Europe as a representative to the Women's Missionary Society of the African Methodist Conference. "Brown was one of the first to become interested in the formation of Black woman's clubs…she supported the cause of woman suffrage, which she first espoused while a student at Wilberforce when she heard Susan B. Anthony speak."[172] Brown served as president of the Ohio Federation of Colored Women's Clubs from 1905 to 1912 and served as the president of the National Association of Colored Women from 1920 to 1924. During the 1920s and 1930s, Brown published several works including *Tales My Father Told* (1925) and *Homespun Heroines and Other Women of Distinction* (1926). Self-published from Homewood Cottage, Brown's home at Wilberforce, *Tales My Father Told* recounts Thomas Brown's adventures as a conductor on the Underground Railroad. *Homespun Heroines* is a volume of sixty biographies of African American women, compiled, written and edited by Brown. She wrote twenty-eight of the essays herself, including one about her mother Frances Jane Brown. Brown never married or had any children and spent the rest of her educational and professional career and life at Wilberforce University. She died there 16 September 1949.

Fannie Barrier Williams was born 12 February 1855, in Brockport, New York to Anthony J. Barrier and Harriet Prince Barrier. The Barrier family was a member of the Black Upper-Middle-Class Social Elite. "My parents and grandparents were free people. My mother was born in New York State and my father in Pennsylvania. They both attended common schools and were fairly educated."[173] The Barrier family's class status was conferred by birthright and professional and financial success; Anthony Barrier was a prosperous barber and coal merchant. He was also a popular community leader in the predominantly white community in which the Barrier family lived. "We suffered from no discriminations on account of color or "previous condition," and lived in blissful ignorance of the fact that we were practicing the unpardonable sin of "social equality." "[174] Fannie Williams' sheltered and affluent childhood had taught her that the rights and respectability of 'true womanhood' were *naturally* hers to claim. Her upbringing also taught her that equal treatment and harmonious living among Black and white Americans was not only possible but also *natural*. "It seemed all a simple part of the natural life we lived where people are loved and respected for their worth in spite of their darker complexions."[175]

In 1870, Williams graduated from the State Normal School at Brockport. Soon thereafter, she joined the exodus of teachers from the north traveling to the south in order to teach in the newly emancipated Black community. There, for the first time, Williams had to confront and navigate the racism, discrimination, and segregation of the south. "…I have never quite recovered from the shock and pain of my first bitter realization that to be a colored woman is to be discredited, mistrusted and often meanly hated."[176] After spending several years in the south, Williams accepted a teaching position in Washington, D.C. where she also studied art. Then became a student at the New England Conservatory of Music. There Williams experienced northern racism and discrimination. "It is scarcely possible to enumerate the many ways in which an ambitious colored young woman is prevented from being all that she might be in the higher directions of life in this country."[177]

While in Washington, Williams met and eventually married a young attorney named S. Laing Williams (1887). As in her girlhood, Williams's married life was one of privilege and uncommon social access. She participated in a myriad of social welfare reform 'programs' in an integrated environment "…on a common basis of fellowship and helpfulness…I experienced very few evidences of race prejudice…"[178] Williams's earlier experiences with the triad of oppression south and north, however, had forever opened her eyes to how American society viewed all African American women. "Kindness to me as an individual did not satisfy me or blind me to the many inequalities suffered by young colored women seeking employment and other advantages of metropolitan life."[179] Williams's experiences also forced her to reevaluate her beliefs about the dynamics of her social interaction and relationships with white women. "I soon discovered that it was much easier for progressive white women to be considerate and even companionable to one colored woman whom they chanced to know and like than to be just and generous to colored women as a race who needed their sympathy and influence in securing employment and recognition..."[180]

Williams's dramatically different girlhood and adult experiences with race, gender and class served to convince her that the only way for Black women to gain recognition from the larger community of their innate respectability and dignity was through unfettered educational and economic opportunity. While some of her Black Victorian Feminist peers focused on gaining better educational opportunity for Black women, Williams focused her attention on using her "...influence and associations to further the cause of these helpless young colored women, in an effort to save themselves and society, by finding, for those who must work, suitable employment."[181]

In 1894, Williams was nominated for membership in the elite, and all white, Chicago Women's Club. An uproar immediately ensued. A faction within this self-proclaimed 'progressive' club bitterly fought against the acceptance of Williams. She later recounted: "...every phase of my public and private life was scrutinized and commented upon in an vain effort to find something in proof of my ineligibility."[182] Some members contacted Williams and informed her that if she was admitted they would resign their memberships: "they did not think that time had yet come for that sort of equality."[183] After fourteen months of debate, according to Williams: "the common sense of the members finally prevailed over their prejudices. When the final vote was taken I was elected to membership by a decisive majority."[184]

Williams was a dedicated welfare reformer. Keenly aware of the lack of Black physicians and nurses in hospitals, she was instrumental in the establishment of Provident Hospital in 1891. This interracial medical facility included a training school for nurses that admitted Black women. Williams participated in the foundation of the National League of Colored Women (1893) and was likewise involved with the club's next incarnation—the National Association of Colored Women (1896). These women's clubs provided kindergartens, mothers' support groups, childcare centers, employment bureaus, and saving banks for Black women. In 1895, she established the National Federation of Afro-American Women. She was chairperson of the committee on state schools for dependant children of the Illinois Woman's Alliance; was a founder and corresponding secretary of the board of directors of the Phyllis Wheatley Home Association and director of the art and music department for the Prudence Crandall Study Club (a literary society formed by the elite of the Black community in Chicago, Illinois).

Williams was also the Chicago correspondent for the *Woman's Era*—the first newspaper about, by, and for African American women. This monthly magazine "informed subscribers about fashion, health, family life and legislation. Women from Chicago, Kansas City, Washington, Denver, New Orleans, and New York contributed to the magazine and served as heads of the magazine's departments."[185] Williams co-authored the book *A New Negro for A New Century*. This book detailed the work and achievements accomplished by the nineteenth century Black movement. In it, Williams provided a historical account of the Black women's club movement and provided an extensive nationwide listing of Black women's clubs and organizations. "The club movement among colored women reaches the sub-social condition of the entire race…the club is only one of many means for the social uplift of a race."[186] After the death of her husband, in 1921, Williams remained in Chicago for five more years, continuing her reform work. In 1926, she returned to Brockport, New York to live with her sister. There she continued to agitate for the uplift of the Black community and the elevation of Black womanhood until her death in 1944.

Anna Julia Haywood Cooper was born 10 August 1858, in Raleigh, North Carolina, to Hannah Stanley and the man who enslaved her, George Washington Haywood. Cooper and her mother gained their emancipation with the end of the Civil War. When she was seven years old, Cooper was admitted to St. Augustine's Normal School and Collegiate Institute, in Raleigh. Founded under the auspices of the Protestant Episcopal Church, the purpose of the school was to "…educate teachers of both sexes for the instruction of the colored people in the south."[187] By the next year Cooper proved to be such an excellent student that she was appointed as a student teacher "…having to stand on a chair to reach the blackboard." For her services she received a $100 yearly stipend."[188] Cooper's thirst for knowledge was insatiable: "I had devoured what was put before me, and, like Oliver Twist was looking around to ask for more. I constantly felt (as I suppose many an ambitious girl has felt) a thumping from within…"[189]

Following her quest for knowledge, Cooper wrote a letter to President Fairchild, of Oberlin College, detailing her academic achievements in the hopes of gaining admission "…beside the English branches, Latin: Caesar, seven books; Virgil's Aeneid, six books; Sallust's Cataline and Jugurtha; and a few orations of Cicero—Greek; White's First Lessons; Goodwin's Greek Reader, containing selections from Xenophan, Plato, Herodotus and Thucydides; and five or six books of the Iliad;—Mathematics: Algebra and Geometry entire…I am extremely anxious to accomplish this long cherished wish, and will feel grateful for any kindly interest taken in my behalf."[190] She was promptly admitted to the sophomore class.

In 1881, Cooper enrolled in the four year 'gentleman's course' at Oberlin College and when she graduated in 1884 she was among the first African American women to do so. After graduation, Cooper taught modern languages at Wilberforce University. From 1885–1887 she taught mathematics, Latin and German at Oberlin College while simultaneously earning a Masters degree in Mathematics (1887). In early 1887 Cooper returned to St. Augustine's and, later that year, married George A.G. Cooper—an Episcopal theology student from Nassau, British West Indies, a Greek teacher at St. Augustine's. Sadly, she was widowed two years later. Then, in 1889, Cooper accepted a position teaching Latin and math at the M Street High School in Washington, D.C. The M Street High School was the largest of its kind for African American youth in the country. Its curriculum "…essentially preparatory designed to prepare promising students as teachers and leaders."[191] In 1892, Cooper published *A Voice From the South By a Black Woman From the South.*

In 1902, Cooper was appointed principal of the M Street High School in Washington, D.C. (where she had occupied a teaching position since 1887). The M Street High School was a college preparatory school whose curriculum was centered on classical studies. During her tenure as principal, Cooper developed and executed a high standard of scholastic expectation and achievement for her students. She sought and hired a teaching staff that was as dedicated as she to the preparation of the student body to pass college entrance exams and to eventually occupy positions of leadership in the Black community. Cooper's greatest achievement as principal was realized when she gained accreditation for the M Street High School from Ivy League Universities. Harvard, Yale, Brown and Oberlin all admitted graduates from the high school.

From 1906 to 1910, Cooper occupied the chair of languages—French, German, Latin and Greek—at Lincoln University in Jefferson City, Missouri. In 1910, she returned to M Street High School as a teacher of Latin. At that point in her life, Cooper decided to matriculate for a PhD. For the next three summers (1911–1913) she studied French Literature, history and phonetics at the Guilde Internationale in Paris, France. The next four summers (1913–1917) were devoted to fulfilling course requirements at Columbia University in New York City. In 1917, Cooper completed her dissertation, a college edition of the eleventh century epic *Plerinage de Charlemangne.* Three summers of study in Paris, however, had "given her a new direction to her choice of a field of specialization as well as the experience of living in a community free of race consciousness."[192]

Cooper decided to transfer her class credits from Columbia University to the Sorbonne and matriculate for her doctorate at the University of Paris; necessitating "the writing of a new dissertation on a subject approved by the French institution."[193] Her new dissertation, *The Attitude of France toward Slavery during the Revolution*, explored and discussed the slave revolt in the French colony of Saint Dominique in 1791. On 23 March 1925, Cooper defended her dissertation at the University of Paris. *The Diplome de Docteur es lettres de la Faculte de Paris* was awarded afterward—Anna Julia Cooper was sixty-six years old. Cooper returned to her teaching position at the M Street High School, now named Dunbar High School, where she remained until her retirement in 1930.

That same year Cooper became a teacher and administrator at the Grelinghuysen Group of Schools for Employed Colored Persons in Washington, D.C. Frelinghuysen University's mission was to provide educational opportunity to "the group lowest down, the intentionally forgotten man, untaught and unprovided for either in the public schools for all classes or in the colleges and universities for the talented tenth [and] to promote harmonious relations between whites and colored citizens…"[194] Unfortunately, lack of accreditation and financial hardship forced the school to close in 1961. This time, Cooper retired for good. On 27 February 1964, Dr. Anna Julia Cooper died in her home in Washington—she was 107 years old.

Ida Bell Wells was born 16 July 1862 in Holly Springs, Mississippi to Jim and Lizzie (Warrenton) Wells. Jim Wells, born enslaved, was the son of an enslaved woman named Peggy and the man who enslaved her. Mr. Wells was trained as a carpenter and apprenticed to a white contractor. On this plantation Jim Wells met Lizzie Warrenton. Ms. Warrenton, also born enslaved and sold away from her family, worked as a cook on the plantation. As soon as they were emancipated Jim and Lizzie Wells were married and elected to remain in Holly Springs. The Wells sent all of their children to school "I do not remember when or where I started school…Our job was to go to school and learn all we could."[195] When Ida Wells was sixteen years old a Yellow Fever epidemic devastated the population of Holly Springs; during which she lost her parents and took full responsibility of her five siblings. Wells supported her family by teaching at a nearby school. "I then found a woman who had been an old friend of my mother to stay at the house with the children while I went out to my country school to teach. I came home every Friday afternoon, riding the six miles on the back of a big mule. I spent Saturday and Sunday washing, ironing and cooking for the children and went back to my country school on Sunday afternoon."[196] In 1879, Wells was invited to live with her aunt Fannie Butler in Memphis, Tennessee. Taking two siblings with her and leaving three behind with relatives, Wells accepted her aunt's offer, moved to Memphis and procured a better paying teaching position in the Shelby County school district.

Now, instead of riding a mule to and from home and school, Wells rode the train. One day in 1884, when she boarded the train and sat in the 'ladies coach' the conductor instructed her to move to the smoking/men's car, the newly desig-nated segregated area for African Americans, Wells refused: "He tried to drag me out of the seat but the moment he caught hold of my arm I fastened my teeth in the back of his hand. I had braced my feet against the seat in front and was hold-ing to the back…[the conductor] went forward and got the baggage-man and another man to help him and of course they succeeded in dragging me out. They were encouraged to do this by the attitude of the white ladies and gentlemen in the car; some of them even stood on the seats so that they could get a good view and continue applauding the conductor for his brave stand."[197] Wells sued the Chesapeake and Ohio Railroad, won and was awarded five-hundred dollars; but the state supreme court later reversed the lower court's ruling.

"I had always been a voracious reader…I had formed my ideals on the best Dicken's stories, Louisa May Alcott's, Mrs. A.D.T. Whitney's, and Charlotte Bronte's books, and Oliver Optics stories for boys. I had read the bible and Shakespeare through, but I had never read a Negro book or anything about Negroes…I knew nothing about life except what I had read."[198] While teaching in the Memphis public school system, Wells joined a lyceum of educational and intellectual peers who met every Friday afternoon to participate in literary recita-tions and debates: "It was the breath of life to me…"[199] At these meetings Wells met and befriended several members of the Memphis Black intelligentsia and, augmented by her participation in the African American community's school sys-tem, began to form her own opinions of African American life.

By 1887, Wells' literary talent, along with participation in the lyceum, had garnered her the positions of editor of and journalist for the *Evening Star*—a weekly newspaper that was a main source of information and communication for the Memphis Black community—and journalist for the *Living Way*—a 'Black periodical' published by a local Baptist church. "I had observed and thought much about the conditions as I had seen them in the country schools and churches. I had an instinctive feeling that the people who had little or no school training should have something coming into their homes weekly which dealt with their problems in a simple, helpful way. So…I wrote in a plain common-sense way on the things which concerned our people...It was not long before these articles were copied and commented on by other Negro newspapers in the country, and I received letters from other editors inviting me to write for them."[200] In 1889, she bought a third interest in the Memphis *Free Speech* and *Headlight*; soon thereafter she became the editor of both newspapers. "...I felt that I had at last found my real vocation..."[201] Wells further co-mingled her work as an educator and journalist, writing articles about the condition of Black schools, contending that inadequate supplies and poorly trained teachers contributed to the substandard education of Black children. After her articles ran, the white school board did not renew Wells's contract, thus unwittingly providing the opportunity for her to focus all of her attention on activism via journalism.

"While I was thus carrying on the work of my newspaper, happy in the thought that our influence was helpful and that I was doing the work I loved and had proved that I could make a living out of it, there came the lynching in Memphis which changed the whole course of my life."[202] In 1892, three Black male peers, Thomas Moss, Calvin McDowell, and Henry Steward were lynched. Moss, McDowell and Steward owned and operated a successful grocery store that served the Memphis Black community. The white owner of a competing grocery store had them arrested for 'conspiracy'; as a result the Black and white Memphis communities clashed and Moss, McDowell, and Steward were arrested and charged with 'inciting a riot'. Soon thereafter, the three men were taken from their jail cells, shot and hanged by a white mob. Until that incident, Wells had believed in the social lie that lynching was reserved for rapists, specifically the crime of a Black man raping a white woman. Moss, McDowell and Steward, however, had not been accused of raping white women. "This is what opened my eyes to what lynching really was. An excuse to get rid of Negroes who were acquiring wealth and prosperity and thus keep the race terrorized and 'keep the nigger down'.[203]

Wells channeled her grief, fear and rage into her newspapers' editorial column. She and other community leaders urged those of the Memphis Black community to move west. Thus, began a mass exodus of African Americans:

> "For the first time in their lives the white people of Memphis had seen earnest, united action by Negroes which upset the economic and business conditions. They had thought the excitement would die down; that Negroes would forget and become again, as before, the wealth producers of the South—the hewers of wood and drawers of water, the servants of white men. But the excitement was kept up, the colored people continued to leave, business remained at a standstill, and there was still a dearth of servants to cook their meals and wash their clothes and keep their homes in order, to nurse their babies and wait on

their tables, to build their homes and do all classes of laborious work...The whites had killed the goose that laid the golden egg of Memphis prosperity and Negro contentment; yet they were amazed that colored people continued to leave the city by scores and hundreds."[204]

Furthermore, this horrible crime spurred Wells to investigate the true circumstances behind individual cases of lynching. "I stumbled on the amazing record that every case of rape reported in that three months became such only when it became public...The more I studied the situation, the more I was convinced that the Southerner had never gotten over the resentment that the Negro was no longer his plaything, his servant, and his source of income."[205]

Long before the lynching of her friends, Wells had accepted an invitation extended to her by Frances Harper to attend the A.M.E. general conference in Philadelphia, Pennsylvania in May 1892. Wells also decided to accept an invitation from the editor of the *New York Age*—T. Thomas Fortune, to visit New York City immediately following the conference. So, after writing and submitting a week's worth of editorial articles concerning her lynch law expose to the *Free Speech* Wells left for her eastern trip. In so doing she unwittingly saved her own life. While Wells was in New York City the Memphis *Free Speech* ran one of her editorials, that read in part: "Nobody in this section believes the old threadbare lie that Negro men assault white women. If Southern men are not careful they will over-reach themselves and a conclusion will be reached which will be very damaging to the moral reputation of their women."[206] Three days after Wells' editorial ran a 'committee' of white Memphis citizens burned down the offices of the *Free Speech*, ran the business manager J.L. Fleming out of town, and left notice that "...anyone trying to publish the paper again would be punished with death."[207]

T. Thomas Fortune invited Wells to join the staff at the *New York Age* and continue her expose on lynch law in America, she accepted. "Having lost my paper, had a price put on my life, and been made an exile from home for hinting at the truth, I felt that I owed it to myself and to my race to tell the whole truth now that I was where I could do so freely."[208] In October 1892, Wells' investigative research culminated with an in-depth feature story entitled "Southern Horrors: Lynch Law and All Its Phases." Two months after the expose was published, according to Wells: "Two colored women remarked on my revelations during a visit with each other and said they thought that the women of New York and Brooklyn should do something to show appreciation of my work and to protest the treatment which I had received."[209] One of these women was Victoria Earle Matthews, a fellow journalist at the *New York Age* and a staunch Black Victorian

Feminist. Matthews organized and raised funds for a 'public testimonial' that Wells would deliver at Lyric Hall in New York City on October 5, 1892, inviting like-minded Black women from Boston, Philadelphia and New York.

Wells's testimony began with the tragic and horrific lynching of Moss, McDowell and Steward. She then detailed her involvement with the mass Black exodus from Memphis after the lynchings, her subsequent investigation into the whys and wherefores of America's lynch law, and the events leading up to her exile. The response to Wells' testimonial was extremely positive and generated three important results. "First, it was the beginning of the club movement among the colored women in the country."[210] Second, Wells's testimonial marked the beginning of her public speaking career. The positive response she received from her appearance at Lyric Hall garnered her public speaking invitations in Philadelphia, Wilmington, Delaware, Chester, Pennsylvania, and Washington D.C. "…The third great result of that wonderful testimonial…resulted in an invitation to England and the beginning of a worldwide campaign against lynching."[211]

After the Exposition concluded, Wells remained in Chicago. On 24 June 1895, she married F.L. Barnett—an attorney and owner of the *Chicago Conservator* (Chicago's first Black owned newspaper). Barnett was also a widower with two children, he and Wells had four more children. Her strongest supporter, Barnett encouraged his wife to "continue her antilynching and political activities…often traveling with one or more children, she was persistent in speaking to groups about lynching and other reform activities."[212] In addition to motherhood, writing, being a journalist for the *Chicago Conservator*, and her antilynching campaign activities, for five years Wells served as president of the Ida B. Wells Club, established in Chicago, Illinois' the first Black orchestra and opened the first Black kindergarten there.

In 1910, Wells opened the Negro Fellowship League—an organization that provided "lodging, recreation facilities, a reading room, and employment for Black migrant males."[213] In 1913, she formed the first Black female suffrage club in Illinois—the Alpha Suffrage Club. "I had been a member of the Women's Suffrage Association…when I saw that we were likely to have a restricted suffrage, and the white women of the organization were working like beavers to bring it about, I made another effort to get our women interested."[214] For the rest of her life, Wells continued her antilynching campaign and reform work. Ida B. Wells-Barnett died of Uremia (a kidney disease) in Chicago in 1931.

Intersections Among These Revolutionary Petunias

At this hour when a thousand social ills beset her, she is taking hold of life in a serious and helpful spirit. It is becoming more and more evident that she is not afraid of the age in which she lives nor its problems...She will some day become the heart and the very life of everything that is best amongst us.

—Fannie Barrier Williams, *The Colored Girl*

These seven women's lives encompassed seventy years of a tumultuous time in Black history. One of the many unique traits that these women shared was their ability to enact resistance and activism through unconventional means and *conventional means unconventionally*. Through the vehicles of church work, writing/publishing, and unconventional aspirations and occupations, these seven women were illustrative of how the triad of oppression informed and shaped their lives and activism, and how their lives and activism are representative examples of Black Victorian Feminist theory and methodology. I combine certain experiences of Brown, Cooper, Coppin, Early, Harper, Wells and Williams in order to provide a nuanced analysis of how the social forces of nineteenth century Black exterior, interior and alternative realities reveal the roots of the Black Victorian Feminist perspective.

Sarah Jane Early and Fannie Jackson Coppin expressed and promoted the Black Victorian Feminist ethic through the vehicle of the Black church. One of the cornerstones of the nineteenth century Black community was the Black church. This institution was established in response to the pervasive prejudice and discrimination experienced by African Americans at the hands of white church leaders and their congregations. The Black church, regardless of denomination, represented the physical, psychic, and spiritual center of the Black community. Between 1816 and 1852, for example, the African Methodist Episcopalian church's membership grew remarkably and Black women were the majority participants in that expansion. African American women in general, Black Victorian Feminists in particular, played a pivotal role in the Black Church. Black women "...were crucial to broadening the public arm of the church and making it the most powerful institution of racial self-help in the African American community."[215] Black Victorian Feminists had little access to aldermen and congressmen; few opportunities to attend White House conferences or correspond with Supreme Court justices in order to lobby for government programs beneficial to the Black community. Through their participation in the church they focused on building private institutions in order to provide for their community what the 'white state' would not. "Thus a large proportion of their political energy went to raising money, and under the most difficult of circumstances—trying to collect from the poor and the limited middle class to help the poor."[216] Through their efforts, Black Victorian Feminists raised enough money to build and sustain churches, schools and homes for the elderly, hospitals, orphanages, and a myriad of other social welfare services to the Black community.

Most importantly, however, Sarah Jane Early and Fannie Jackson Coppin worked within the orthodoxy of the Black church to agitate for the recognition of women's rightful leadership role in the church. Sarah Jane Early began her activist career when the Black church was still in its infancy. In 1893 she discussed how Black women were not only members of the church but had been involved in every aspect of the early struggle to establish the Black church: "In the early days of the Church when its ministers were illiterate and humble, and her struggles with poverty and proscription were long and severe…the women were ready, with their time, their talent, their influence and their money, to dedicate all to the upbuilding of the Church."[217] Early went on to detail how Black women not only raised money to build Black churches, and/or opened their homes for church services, but also paid the ministers' salaries. In the early days of the church Black women openly assisted or presided over prayer meetings and Sabbath schools as well as provided lodging for visiting preachers and their families. Early reminded her readers that Black women provided these services, while continuing to work and take care of their families, because they were as dedicated as Black men to building a strong Black church. But Black women were also active in and supported the church, according to Early, because "…the freedom which they enjoyed in their worship and the satisfaction arising from equal rights in church privileges made the work more precious and secured to them greater hope for future success."

Fannie Jackson Coppin began her activist career when the Black church was a firmly established Black community institution. By this time, however, it appears that Black women were not experiencing the freedom of worship and satisfaction arising from equal rights in church privileges that was indicative of Early's and Black women's experience during the eighteenth and early nineteenth centuries. In 1888, while attending a missionary conference in London, England, Coppin was admonished by a Presbyterian minister not to assume any ecclesiastical functions. Coppin later said "This got me riled and in reply I tried to make it plain that the Lord God alone gives limit to the functions of woman's religious work."[218] Later in the day when Coppin was invited to address the conference, she gave a brief but eloquent address on the subject of women's role in the church:

> "…and it may very well be said of women, that while they are and were created second, they were not only created with body, but they were created also with a head, and they are responsible therefore to decide in certain matters and to use their own judgment. It is also very true…that fools often rush in where angels fear to tread; but then I question as to whether all fools are confined to the feminine gender."[219]

Sarah Jane Early and Fanny Jackson Coppin not only worked within the orthodoxy of the Black church to agitate for the recognition of women's rightful leadership role in the church, through their lives and rhetoric they served to further subvert the foundational tenets of the cult of true womanhood. They challenged the silent, meek helpmate of women's church work. They asserted, from a woman-centered context, that Black women were as equally obligated as Black men to uplift themselves, the Black community, and the Black church.

Anna Julia Cooper, Ida B. Wells and Hallie Quinn Brown expressed and promoted the Black Victorian Feminist ethic through the vehicle of writing from which they confronted and debunked the larger society's nineteenth century gender constructions of Black womanhood and Black manhood. Hailed as the first Black feminist publication, *A Voice from the South, By a Black Woman from the South* is a collection of nine essays written by Cooper between 1886 and 1892. Cooper's seminal work encapsulates the essence of Black Victorian Feminism, primarily, in two ways: she casts the voice of the Black woman into the foreground of intellectual, political and cultural discussion; and she makes the case for the existence and validity of an insurgent alternate conception of true womanhood.

In casting Black women into the foreground, Cooper provides a context that clearly illuminates the unique position of Black women in nineteenth century America. The late nineteenth century represented an exceptional moment in Black women's history, in particular, and American history at large. The Slaveocracy was in tatters and the end of that regime had implications that would soon spread across the globe. In short, the feudal/agricultural system was a relic of the past. Industry was the engine of the future. On its face, the country was amidst a time of change and progress. Just under the surface, however, a cultural revolution was also being waged. The rise of Jim/Jane Crow was the literal and figurative representation of political, economic and social oppression against which a *new* class of African American was struggling: "…preparing the way for transitions from the rural South to the urban North, from the culture of southern folk-ways to the urban ways of the new middle classes…"[220] And in the midst of it all, Black women "…were raising in significant numbers to positions of prominence and relative power."[221] Through her "…formulation [and implementation of] the notion that intellectual work ought to be an archaeological discovery of the unique in social life…," Cooper not only rendered the nineteenth century Black woman visible to the larger society and Black men, she gave notice to one and all that Black womanhood was a force to be reckoned with.[222]

Charles Lemert remarks that one of the most common criticisms of Cooper's work, from twentieth and twenty-first century Black feminists and historians, is that she "…all too comfortably accepted the white pieties of the true womanhood ideal."[223] I submit that Cooper was not so much wedded to the ideals of the cult of true womanhood but was committed to creating and promulgating an intellectual and cultural space for Black women—and from within this space the true breadth and depth of Black women's voices and experiences could be discovered, exchanged and debated. Moreover, to fault Cooper for voicing a seemingly non-twenty-first-century-feminist worldview not only takes Cooper's life and works out of context, it yet again reduces Black women's experiences and voices to the homogeneous and one dimensional.

Cooper believed in and was staunchly loyal to nineteenth century ideals of piety and domesticity because they were not solely the ideals held by the larger society, but were held by the Black community as well. Additionally, when one considers how she lived her life it is quite apparent that her ideal of true womanhood bore little resemblance to that of the cult of true womanhood. Cooper accomplished truly *brilliant* feats of academic achievement and was a refined and cultured woman (two facts that were an anthem to the larger society's construction of race, gender, and class). The most important factor of her life, however, was that she was a completely self-sufficient woman. Cooper purchased, furnished, and maintained three homes (in her lifetime); supported her mother, traveled to Europe; and raised six foster children as a *single woman*. She pursued her teaching profession and intellectual pursuits her *entire life* without the financial support of a husband—and her annual income never exceeded $1,800![224] Every middle class advantage she enjoyed, every scrap of knowledge she acquired, every dollar she spent was earned entirely on her own. Yes, Cooper was a typical Black Victorian Feminist. By that I mean that she verdantly believed in and adhered to an ideology of respectability while simultaneously honing a superior intellect, financially supporting her family, working mightily for racial uplift, and authoring a quintessential book that defined the unique position of the nineteenth century woman in American history from an "...acutely self-conscious understanding of the Black woman in American political and cultural life."[225]

The Black woman, according to Cooper, in her *role as mother*, was an essential element to a civilization's advancement and the uplift of the race because "...it is she who must form man by directing the earliest impulses of his character."[226] On its face such a declaration may lead one to think that Cooper was referring to the traditional ideology of the 'cult of true womanhood.' I contend, however, that this was not the case. It is important to remember that Cooper was born only two years before the beginning of the Civil War. Cooper's earliest childhood years, then, were spent amidst the dangers and horrors of war; all under the oppressive fist of slavery. By the end of the Civil War North Carolina had suffered the largest loss of life, due to battles and disease, of all the Confederate States.[227] It's amazing that a child-slave survived, but Cooper did—and her mother was the reason why. Moreover, Cooper intimates that her survival and life's accomplishments had everything to do with her mother, Hannah Stanley, and nothing to do with the man who had enslaved her and her mother—Cooper's father. She denied "...any indebtedness to my white father beyond the fact of [my] existence." Of her mother, Cooper declared: "[her] self-sacrificing toil to give me advantages she never enjoyed herself is worthy of the highest praise and undying gratitude."[228] It is safe to assume that Hannah Stanley was instrumental in enrolling her then six-year-old daughter at the Institute and encouraging her daughter's intellectual development. At a time and place in history when only one year previous laws against teaching a slave to read "...were harsh and penalties for violation severe," Hannah Stanley's enrollment of her daughter and life long encouragement of her daughter's potential was truly a resistant and revolutionary act. An enslaved woman raised Anna Julia Cooper, who was herself enslaved. Thus, her self-defined notions of motherhood were crucially informed by an alternate understanding of the role that motherhood could and did play in the enslaved women's community. Mothers were the ones who fought for the economic continuity and survival of their families. Furthermore, even after emancipation, Black women continued to operate from this alternate understanding of motherhood. Thus, Black women were the movers, the doers, and the actors not passive submissive responders—a fundamental tenet of the 'cult of true womanhood.' When regarded from this vantage point, Cooper's contention that motherhood was a vital element in the regeneration and progression of civilization and the African American community is radical: "The training of children is a task on which an infinity of weal or woe depends...It is a matter of small moment, it seems to me, whether that lovely girl in whose accomplishments you take such pride and delight, can enter the gay and crowded salon with the ease and elegance of this or that French or English gentlewoman, compared with the decision as to whether her individuality is going to reinforce the good or evil elements of the world."[229]

Cooper was not solely a Black Victorian Feminist in theory but in action. While much has been written and said about her life-long career commitment to securing educational opportunities for African Americans in general, I believe that not enough attention has been given to her equal dedication to securing educational opportunities for Black women. It was Cooper's contention that academic achievement for Black women could only assist in the elevation of Black womanhood, the 'uplift of the race,' and the advancement of civilization. "Religion, science, art, economics have all needed the feminine flavor; and literature, the expression of what is permanent and best in all of these, may be gauged at any time to measure the strength of the feminine ingredient."[230] Moreover, academic achievement did not render Black women unfit for true womanhood but rendered the traditional ideal of the 'cult of true womanhood' as *unfit for Black women*! Cooper derided the traditional conception of "...the idea that women may stand on pedestals or live in doll houses (if they happen to have them) but they must not furrow their brows with thought or attempt to help men tug at the great questions of the world."[231]

Cooper, and other proponents of focusing on classical education and academic achievement, supported the idea that industrial training was important to the economic stability of the Black community. But for the Black student who showed aptitude, however, "...every effort should be made to secure the opportunity for higher education to enable them to become teachers and leaders of their race."[232] She eschewed the contention that industrial training was a more 'realistic' and 'appropriate' educational sphere for African Americans than a classical education. For Black women especially, she believed that possession of a higher education was essential, not only for the elevation of Black womanhood but for racial uplift: "...if there is an ambitious girl with pluck and brain to take the higher education, encourage her to make the most of it. The earnest well trained Christian young woman, as a teacher, as a home-maker, as wife, mother, or silent influence even, is as potent a missionary agent among our people...and I claim that at the present stage of our development in the South she is ever more important and necessary."[233]

In *A Voice from the South* Cooper speaks to two audiences interchangeably: the larger society and Black men, and Black women. To the first audience, Cooper excavates the unique life and voice of nineteenth century Black women, casting them into the foreground of the American consciousness—lifting the veil of invisibility, solidly displacing negative and degrading cultural images of Black womanhood, and declaring that *true Black womanhood* was a force to be reckoned with. To the second audience, *A Voice from the South* is a seminal and priceless work of intellectual art that makes it quite clear, I contend, that Cooper, and Black Victorian Feminists at large, did *not* comfortably accept the pieties of the idealized cult of true womanhood. Cooper brilliantly appropriates, subverts and manipulates the larger society's constructions of race, gender and class that had an iron-gripped stranglehold on American intellectual and cultural production. Moreover, this stranglehold intimately touched each and every aspect of nineteenth century Black women's lives. Moreover, even an tangential allegiance by Black women to the ideal of true womanhood could not cloud nor sever the real connections between the derogatory construction of Black womanhood and the oppression of African Americans as a group. Thus, Cooper's re-construction of Black womanhood was not only a personal revolutionary act but was a warning and a call to arms for every African American, Black women in particular: "No other hand can move the lever. She must be loosed from her hands and set to work…[and] every attempt to elevate the Negro…cannot but prove abortive unless so directed as to utilize the indispensable agency of an elevated and trained womanhood…Only the BLACK WOMAN can say 'when and where I enter, in the quiet, undisputed dignity of my womanhood, without violence…then and there the whole Negro race enters with me'."[234]

Even before the editorial that resulted in her exile from Memphis was published, Ida B. Wells had done much to attract the attention of the white Memphis community. In addition to her public and prominent participation in the Memphis Black exodus and boycott, in every edition of the *Free Speech* Wells published an editorial or article that served to continue her one-woman crusade not to allow the white community to forget the atrocities committed against her three friends nor allow them to ignore the continuing injustice done to the victims, their families and the Black community—embodied in the dogged refusal, by the powers that be, to bring the murders to trial. Wells was well aware that the same people, and their supporters, who had murdered her friends would eventually turn their attention to the Black journalist who refused to let their crime fade from the public conscious. Vowing to "…sell my life as dearly as possible if I was attacked," Wells purchased a pistol to protect herself: "I felt that one had better die fighting against injustice than to die like a dog or a rat in a trap…I felt if I could take one lyncher with me, this would even up the score a little bit. But fate decided the blow should fall when I was away…"[235] Five months after the offices of the *Free Speech* was firebombed and Wells accepted a part owner and full editor position at the *New York Age*, she published the results of her investigation into America's 'Lynch Law.' In October 1892, Wells' investigative research culminated with an in-depth feature story entitled "Southern Horrors: Lynch Law and All Its Phases." The seven-column article appeared on the front page of the *New York Age*; providing a detailed accounting of the dates, places and names of victims lynched for the alleged crime of raping a white woman or child. Moreover, Wells contended that her in-depth investigation led her to discover the true motivations behind the escalating instances of the lynching of Black men in the South: consensual sexual relationships between white women and Black men and the larger society's unwavering commitment to halting the political, social, and economic advancement of African Americans.

Wells noted that one of the underlying realities of the Slaveocracy was the consensual and non-consensual sexual relationship between white men and Black women. "Such relationships...were notorious...This was so much a fact that such unions had bleached a large percentage of the Negro race, and filled it with the offspring of these unions."[236] Wells went on to remark on the intricate hypocrisies embedded in antebellum and post-antebellum ideological constructions of gender. "I also found that what the white men of the South practiced as all right for himself, he assumed unthinkable in white women."[237] Antebellum and post-antebellum gender ideology was steeped in Victorian notions of true womanhood. The tenets of the cult of true womanhood had strict guidelines concerning the sexual lives women. In very real ways these tenets were one of the foundational posts of the larger society's conception of self and the world in which they lived and ruled. For the true white woman, her husband, family, friends and neighbors, purity/virginity was her greatest asset. Without it she was not only considered by all to be unnatural but also not a true woman. An obvious observation is that marriage, which was essential for her happiness was "...literally, an end to innocence."[238] Yet, how could a mature woman reconcile the ideological conundrum that nineteenth century moral imperatives of marriage and purity presented?

The contradictions glaringly apparent in this facet of nineteenth century gender ideology was addressed by another—submission. From the moment of her marriage, after she had bestowed her 'greatest treasure' upon her husband (her virginity) "...from that time on [she] was completely dependent upon him, an empty vessel, without legal or emotional existence of her own."[239] Thus, the true white woman was to simply and wholeheartedly submit to her husband's will. For "woman understood her position...She asks for wisdom, constancy, firmness...she is conscious of her inferiority and therefore grateful for the support."[240] Wells's expose revealed a 'dirty little secret' that was extremely troubling to the larger society. The fact that there were white 'true women' who willingly abandoned the gender guidelines of purity and submission to have sexual relationships with Black men threatened not only white male constructions of self but shook the very foundations of a society formed around entrenched ideals of gender, race and class. Thus, Wells contended, the larger society's psyche, in the South and in the North, could not accept the notion that "...there are white women...who love the Afro-American's company even as there are white men notorious for their preference for Afro-American women."[241] Therefore, Wells concluded, whenever a white woman was discovered to have 'fallen in love' with a Black man "...the cry of rape was raised...The many unspeakable and unprintable tortures to which Negro rapists (?) of white women were subjected to were for the purpose of striking terror into the hearts of other Negroes who might be thinking of consorting with *willing* white women."[242] Wells contended that one of the motivations of the lynching of Black men by white mobs was the barbaric reaction of the larger society to the reality of Black male/white female consensual sexual relationships. The second motivation stemmed from the larger society's obsession with halting the political, social and economic advancement of African Americans.

Using statistics, investigating and citing cases compiled by the *Chicago Tribune*, Wells reviewed 728 lynchings that had occurred between 1884 and 1892. Wells found that only one-third of the victims had been charged with rape "...to say nothing of those one-third who were innocent of the charge."[243] Fifty of the victims were lynched for participating in political activities and the rest were murdered for "...all manner of accusations from that of rape of white women, to...being drunk and 'sassy' to white folks."[244] Thus, Wells contended, that those who participated in this crime—and were supported and encouraged by what Wells named a 'malicious and untruthful white press'—were fraudulently shielding themselves behind the threadbare excuse of defending the honor of white women. Wells also identified the larger society as an essential element of the horror embodied in lynch law. Their hands too were stained with the blood of Black victims: "[Those who] disapprove of lynching and remain silent...are participants, criminals, accomplices, accessories before and after the fact, equally guilty with the actual law-breakers who would not persist if they did not know that neither the law nor militia would be employed against them."[245]

Wells ended her brilliant expose with a plan for how the Black community could work to 'repeal' lynch law themselves; the plan was three-fold. First, citing the success of the Memphis Black boycott and exodus, Wells urged Black communities across the nation to effect a 'bloodless revolution:' "The white man's dollar is his god, and to stop this will be to stop outrages in many localities…The appeal to the white man's pocket has ever been more effectual than all the appeals ever made to his conscience."[246] Second, she urged African Americans to defend themselves by any means necessary: "…a Winchester rifle should have a place of honor in every black home, and it should be used for that protection which the law refuses to give."[247] Finally, Wells's investigation proved the complicity of the white press in encouraging and perpetuating the myth of the rabid bestial Black rapist whose favorite prey was the hapless white woman, all the while purposefully obfuscating the fact that "[the] burning alive of black human beings…was done by white men who controlled the forces of law and order in their communities and who could have legally punished rapists and murderers, especially black men who had neither political power nor financial strength with which to evade any justly deserved fate."[248] Thus, the final step in 'repealing' lynch law was for the Black community to support the effort of Black newspapers in putting the true facts behind lynchings before the public, for "…there is no educator to compare with the press."[249]

Gail Bederman's analysis of Wells' expose on Southern Lynch Law revolves around her contention that the primary purpose of late nineteenth century larger society's discourse of civilization revolved around the factors of race, gender and millennial assumptions about human evolutionary progress: "'Civilization,' as turn-of-the-century Americans understood it, simultaneously denoted attributes of race and gender. By invoking the discourse of civilization in a variety of contradictory ways, many Americans found a powerfully effective was to link male dominance to white supremacy."[250] The crux of Bederman's argument is that gender, in this case 'manhood,' is neither an intrinsic essence or a collection of traits but is rather a continual dynamic process through which men claim certain kinds of authority. Nevertheless, according to Bederman, ideologies of gender are not totalizing, they are internally contradictory. "[Thus] because ideologies come into conflict with other ideologies, men and women are able to influence the ongoing ideological processes of gender…They can combine and recombine them, exploit the contradictions between them and work to modify them. They can also alter their position in relation to those ideologies."[251] Bederman identifies Ida B. Wells as one woman who was able to influence the ideological process of gender through manipulation of the nineteenth century larger society's discourse of civilization. She specifically cites Wells' "Southern Horrors: Lynch Law and All Its Phases" and *The Reason Why the Colored American Is Not at the Columbian Exposition* as exemplars of her success in this alteration process.

While I believe that Bederman's analysis is 'right on the money' in regard to her treatment of *The Reason Why*, nineteenth century constructions of race, gender, and class and the Columbian Exposition, I think that she missed the mark with her application of the same theory to "Southern Horrors." The basis of Bederman's analysis of "Southern Horrors" is: one, white Southerners' lynching of African American men was a tool used to bolster white male power and authority; two, media accounts of lynchings, South and North, encouraged Northern white men to identify and align themselves with Southern white men, thus they could all bask in the heady intoxicant of white male power and authority; and, three, Wells's motivation in researching lynch law, publishing her findings, and embarking on a life-long one-woman anti-lynching crusade stemmed from her desire to subvert and manipulate white middle class ideas about race, manhood and civilization to force America to address lynching. Yes, American lynch law was a tool used to bolster white male power and authority. Yes, media depictions of lynching "…encouraged Northern white men to see themselves as manly and powerful and gave them a rich ground on which issues of gender, sexuality, and racial dominance could be attractively combined [packaged] and recombined [repackaged] to depict the overwhelming power of their civilized white manliness."[252] I submit, however, that not only was Wells *not* primarily motivated by a desire to subvert and manipulate nineteenth century white middle class ideologies of gender, race, class—in relation to civilization—her work was *not a subversion or manipulation* of ideologies or anything else.

Bederman's analysis of "Southern Horrors relies heavily on her investigation of the ways and means in which the larger society in the nineteenth century dealt with old and new, always contradictory, "…knowledges about sexuality, manhood, and power."[253] She contends, and I agree, that nineteenth century Victorians were "…obsessed with producing new ways of understanding sex as the key 'truth' about men and women's natures."[254] Moreover, the late nineteenth century escalation of the lynching of Black men purportedly for the crime of raping white women represented one manifestation of how the larger society investigated, discussed, constructed, and re-constructed formulations about the power and authority of manhood and sexuality. Bederman then takes this focus and *superimposes* it onto her analysis of "Southern Horrors." In doing so Bederman investigates one Black woman's experience and intellectual work from the standpoint of what the larger society permitted or prohibited African Americans to do, say, or write. And that standpoint becomes the primary consideration of her analysis—thus obfuscating the true nature of Wells' work by measuring it through the false prism of successful white dominance. In contrast, I contend, displacement of the nineteenth century white man and/or woman from the role of the protagonist in this story and replacing them with Ida B. Wells in the role of the protagonist reveals a fuller, more nuanced understanding of "Southern Horrors."

Wells's motivation behind researching, writing, and publishing "Southern Horrors" begins with her seemingly simple statement: "I felt that I owed it to myself and to my race to tell the whole truth…freely."[255] Certainly, one truth was that white nineteenth century America was, yet *again*, caught in the uncomfortable grip of negotiating the treacherously unstable ground of their gender and race ideologies. But this conflict, and its subversion and manipulation, was not even of secondary concern to Wells. According the Wells, America's lynch law was not merely a manifestation of nineteenth century white America's sexual dysfunction but was yet another tool used to oppress African Americans. "They have cheated him out of his ballot, deprived him of civil rights or redress therefore in the civil courts, robbed him of the fruits of his labor, and are still murdering, burning and lynching him."[256] "Southern Horrors" provides an excellent illustration of how Black Victorian Feminists seamlessly blended their work for the elevation of Black womanhood and the uplift of the Black community. "Southern Horrors" is Wells's personal contribution to this dual endeavor. One often overlooked, and vitally important, part of Wells expose is contained in the final 'chapter:' Self-Help. Here Wells provided a blue print for self and communal empowerment that has nothing to do with white dominance or intra-white ideology formation or re-formation. "The Afro-American can do for himself what no one else can do for him…"[257]

In 1925, at the age of seventy-five, Hallie Quinn Brown published *Homespun Heroines and Other Women of Distinction*. *Homespun Heroines* is a book of biographical essays of sixty African American women whose lives span 184 years of American history (1740–1924). Although Brown personally authored twenty-one of the essays, she enlisted the aid of twenty-eight of her women contemporaries to join in the collaborative effort. *Homespun Heroines* provides precious insight into the life of nineteenth century Black women through presenting the biographies of a group of Black women who were not only talented and accomplished but also incredibly diverse. These women were teachers, nurses, social workers, antislavery activists, homemakers, professional elocutionists, wives, poets, musicians, physicians, mothers, journalists, boarding house proprietors, cake makers, lawyers, church women, maids, quilters, knitters—and many of these women inhabited several of these occupations and professions simultaneously.

Brown provided a detailed analysis of the Black Victorian Feminist alternate conception of true womanhood through the vehicle of the biography. The essay on Sarah Harris Fayerweather (1802–1868) offers one insight into the many layers of Black womanhood. Fayerweather was the wife of a successful blacksmith in the small New England village of Kingston, Rhode Island. She was a middle class wife, mother, and homemaker who also ran a station of the Underground Railroad from her home. As a conductor on the Underground Railroad, Fayerweather's duties entailed: "Safe housing, safe thoroughfare…the procuring of garments for change and disguise, the collection of extra food, the selection of places for hiding and security, last but not least, the proffer of first aid service to weary travelers…"[258] Another exemplar of Black womanhood was Mrs. Jane Roberts (1809–?), the wife of the first African president of Liberia. "Mrs. Roberts graced the Executive Mansion with ease and dignity. She spoke English and French fluently and in all respects was well-bred and refined."[259] In addition to her duties as 'First Lady,' and her cultivation of a personal friendship with Queen Victoria, Mrs. Roberts raised money to build a hospital in Monrovia, Liberia's capitol.

Of course there were biographies of especially distinguished Black women, such as Harriet Tubman. Proudly and reverently referred to as "Moses," "This historic character is in class by herself. She had the skill and boldness of a commander—the courage and strategy of a general. A picturesque figure standing boldly against the commonplace, dark background of a generation in which her lot was cast."[260] Harriet Tubman was a fugitive slave woman who repeatedly returned to the slave South to assist other enslaved African Americans to escape bondage. Tubman first rescued her three brothers, then her parents, and eventually *four hundred other slaves*: "…not one of whom was caught nor did she ever fall into the hands of the enemy, though at one time $12,000 reward was offered for this mysterious 'black ghost.' "[261]

Alongside the biographies of privileged or especially heroic women are the biographies of Black women whose greatest deed was survival. One such woman is Caroline Sherman Andrews-Hill (1888–1914). Hill was born in Columbia County, Tennessee to 'slave' parents. Her father was the foreman of their 'master's' plantation. Her mother, too, was 'favored' and 'highly esteemed.' At a young age Andrews-Hill was given nursemaid duty over the 'master's' children. When her owners learned that Andrews-Hill was learning alongside her charges "prompt measures were taken to prevent her progress in book learning by removing her from the proximity of the schoolroom when her nurselings were reciting their lessons."[262]

In 1848, after her 'master's' family moved them all to Little Rock, Arkansas, Andrews-Hill married Reverend William Wallace Andrews, an educated 'slave' who enjoyed a rare and large amount of personal freedom. After her marriage, Andrews-Hill was allowed to hire herself out, as long as she paid the people who enslaved her for the privilege, and allowed to live in the same house as her husband. For the next fifteen years Andrews-Hill worked and monthly gave the greater part of her wages to her enslavers "...clothed and fed a family of growing children, furnishing all medical attendance needed from time to time at her own expense, and in the last few years of this period paying house rent besides."[263] Since her husband's time was largely spent performing his duties of chief steward and butler to those who enslaved him he was unable to give financial assistance to his family. Andrews-Hill supported them all.

After emancipation, the Andrews worked and saved enough money to buy their own home. Reverend Andrews opened a school in the Methodist church of which he was pastor. "To this school Mrs. Andrews went along with her children...Her burning desire was to learn to read and write fluently. She persevered at home and at school (by long intervals in the latter) until she could read fluently and could write her name."[264] In 1866 Andrews-Hill's life was devastated when her husband and sixteen year old son died seven weeks apart. In 1867 she married Ohmer Hill and the couple: "...wield[ed] a wide influence for good in their community by lives of earnest, honest industry, their example of thrift, and their earnest christian spirit and deed of benevolence to all about them."[265] Caroline Sherman Andrews-Hill did not run a station of the Underground Railroad, 'rub elbows' with royalty, or heroically scout for the Union Army during the Civil War. She was a wife and mother whose greatest goal in life was to learn to read fluently and write her own name. She was "...especially esteemed for her great-hearted warmth and love for all who came to her."[266] Andrews-Hill lived a simple life, she survived, she was an exemplar of Black womanhood.

Homespun Heroines is a historical account of the second phase of Black women's community building endeavors. During the Slaveocracy, enslaved women created and maintained a distinct Black women's community and were vital contributors to the creation and maintenance of the Black 'slave' culture and community. After emancipation, Black women were instrumental in the creation of a post-slavery Black community that was, in part, based in vast female networks created by Black women. Darlene Clark Hines defines this second phase of Black women's community building: "'Making community' means the processes of creating religious, educational, health-care, philanthropic, political, and familial institutions and professional organizations that enabled our people to survive.[267] Moreover, it was through the processes of making community that Black Victorian Feminists, and Black women, were able to re-claim and re-form Black womanhood and create and define a new aesthetic.

What is particularly intriguing about *Homespun Heroines* is that Brown did not intend for her work to be a treatise on Black Victorian Feminist theory and methodology—as Anna Julia Cooper did with *A Voice from the South*, or a crusade to end a particular form of nineteenth century Black oppression, degradation and demoralization—as Ida B. Wells did with "Southern Horrors". Instead, Brown chose to produce an invaluable historical primary source document for *the future study of Black women*: "It is our anxious desire to preserve for future reference an account of these women, their life and character and what they accomplished under the most trying and adverse circumstances..."[268] In addition, Brown intended for her work to be available to future generations of Black women. She wanted to shine an "...instructive light on the struggles endured and the obstacles overcome by our pioneer women."[269] Finally, working from the "settled conviction that something of the kind is needed," Brown and her cohorts of historically self-conscious Black Victorian Feminists determined to chronicle the lives of a broadly diverse group of Black women that illuminated the common elements of nineteenth century Black women's experience (women, wives and mothers trying to secure better lives for themselves and their families) and the uncommon (women who were members of a 'special' group in the American experience, that represented a singular phenomenon with definite characteristics, and the 'baggage' that is necessarily entailed), thereby presenting, for the entire world to see—in the nineteenth century and beyond—the reality of the viable and complex components of Black women's identity.

Homespun Heroines is Brown's contribution to the historicization of Black women's critical involvement in the building of the Black community. Two of the foundational posts of the nineteenth century Black community were the ideological doctrines of self-help and racial solidarity. While the development of the theory and methodology of these interrelated doctrines have been attributed mainly to great nineteenth century 'race men' (i.e. Frederick Douglass and W.E.B. DuBois), Hines contends, and I concur, that: "...it is clear that 'race women' in local Black communities were even more critical to the actual conceptualization and implementation of social welfare programs, the nurturance of oppositional consciousness, and the support of essential institutions."[270] One of the basic goals of African American women's history is to view and treat Black women's lives and experiences as worthy historical subjects, render visible their lives and deeds and ultimately "dramatically advance our understanding of the past and the nature and complexity of American society"[271] *Homespun Heroines* not only accomplishes this endeavor but is tacit proof that the basic goal of African American women's history and its historians, in this case Hallie Quinn Brown, was a historical ongoing process in itself.

Frances Ellen Watkins Harper and Fannie Barrier Williams expressed and promoted the Black Victorian Feminist ethic through the vehicle of the unconventional. "This is a common cause; and if there is any burden to be borne in the Anti-Slavery cause—anything to be done to weaken our hateful chains or assert our manhood and womanhood, I have a right to do my share of the work…if there is common rough work to be done, call on me."[272] Known as the 'brown muse,' Frances Ellen Watkins Harper spent her entire life composing, reciting and publishing poems, fiction, essays and letter that brought the tragic and triumphant story of the nineteenth century Black experience, against the backdrop of a tumultuous time in American history, to the world. In the span of five years, by the time she was thirty years old, Harper was an internationally recognized and lauded journalist and poet. One of the most interesting and unconventional aspects of her life, however, is rarely examined.

Although she was tragically orphaned at the age of three, Harper was raised by a moderately affluent and well-respected free Black family in the slave state of Maryland. She was the rare recipient of a varied, extensive and excellent education. Harper could have easily settled into a life of relative ease and leisure. She could have chosen to avoid and ignore the harsh and ugly reality that the majority of nineteenth century African Americans, enslaved and free, could not escape (physically and mentally). Instead, deciding "…that her personal survival and well-being were intrinsically linked with the survival and well-being of the larger society, and that confrontation, not silence" was the obligation of all who could speak out and act, Harper chose to fully immerse herself into a dangerous and stressful cause—the abolition of slavery.[273]

While nineteenth century life for African Americans was by no means easy, it was uniquely difficult for free African Americans living in 'slave' states. They were an anomalous group, antipathetical to a society that was built—culturally, politically and economically—on the precept that African Americans were inferior sub-human beings fit only for use as chattel. Life, for free African Americans, in such an environment was a delicate and dangerous tight-rope-walk. Nonetheless, in the years directly preceding the Civil War, the lives and well being of free African Americans living in 'slave' states became increasingly precarious. The insurgency of the anti-slavery movement and the increasingly alarming measures by which the United States government attempted to deal with and address this 'peculiar institution' became emblematic of the cultural and economic currents that were simultaneously polarizing the nation and placing free and enslaved African Americans in the eye of the storm. Two legislations, one federal and one state, crucially affected Harper's life and led her to the personal and philosophical revelations that would encourage her to dedicate her life to bringing about radical and revolutionary change.

In 1850, when a twenty-five year old Harper was employed as a domestic and nursemaid; had published her first book of poetry (*Forest Leaves*,) and was writing and publishing pieces in various local periodicals, the United States government passed a legislative package called the Compromise of 1850. Two parts of the legislation, in particular, served to further threaten and oppress African Americans. First, a *compromise* between the pro-slavery and anti-slavery factions in the government decreed that the majority vote of the citizens of new territories would determine whether or not they would enter the Union as free or 'slave' states (remember in the vast majority of states and territories African Americans were largely disenfranchised by law and/or social custom). Second, was a provision called the 'Fugitive Slave Act.' It removed legal authority over fugitive slaves cases from local to federal jurisdiction; required citizens to cooperate with slave-hunters—regardless of whether the state was 'slave' or free—and levied high fines against people caught aiding fugitive slaves. Furthermore, the act established that it "...accepted as proof the ownership signed affidavits from the purported master, but it *denied the alleged slave both the right to a jury trial and the right to testify on her or his own behalf.* (my emphasis)"[274] Finally the law 'sweetened-the-pot' by providing monetary reward that was clearly skewed toward encouraging the false enslavement of free African Americans. Federal commissioners were compensated ten dollars for every fugitive slave claim they ruled to be valid but only five dollars for every claim they denied.[275] Understandably, a large number of free African Americans responded to this 'compromise' by beginning a mass exodus from free and 'slave' states to Canada and the majority of Harper's family joined the exodus.

Instead of joining the exodus, Harper decided to accept a teaching position as the first female teacher at Union Seminary in Ohio (soon the become Wilberforce University). There she taught classes in embroidery and 'plain sewing,' but she quickly left that unrewarding post and accepted another teaching post in Little York, Pennsylvania in 1852. There too Harper was unhappy and unfulfilled. She had a strong desire to participate in the building of Black institutions and the uplift of the Black community, but found that life as a teacher was not her call-ing—but what else was a young, unmarried, educated, ambitious free Black woman to do? In a letter to a friend, Harper summed up her predicament: "What would you do if you were in my place? Would you give up and go back and work at your trade (dress-making)?...The condition of our people, the wants of our children, and the welfare of our race demand the aid of every helping hand..."[276] Shortly thereafter, a law passed in her home state of Maryland, and an incident precipitated by this law, would answer her query.

In 1853, the Maryland state legislature passed a law that, under the penalty of enslavement, forbade free African Americans to enter the state. Later that year a Black man, ignorant of the law, was arrested, sold and sent to Georgia. He escaped, was recaptured and died while in custody. This horrific story was a watershed moment in Harper's life. This one man's story represented, to her, a crystallization of the personal, social and political forces that shaped and informed nineteenth century Black experience. It revealed to Harper the way she could marry her endeavors to aid in the uplift of her community and the larger society, elevate Black womanhood and express her intellectual-self: "Upon that grave...I pledged myself to the Anti-Slavery cause."[277]

Harper, now fortified by and focused on her path, moved to Philadel-phia—the home of the largest and best educated free Black community in the antebellum North. There she lived at a 'station' of the Underground Railroad and for the first time in her life, freely mingled and conversed with fugitive slaves. "To [further] prepare herself for an active abolitionist role, she frequented the office of the local antislavery society, and read avidly on the subject."[278] Harper's new home and circumstance also brought her into close and sustained contact with the best and brightest members of the Black intelligentsia. Naturally, such exposure not only further stimulated her intellectual and creative proclivities but also garnered her publishing contacts and she soon began contributing her writ-ing talents to the Philadelphia based *Christian Recorder*, the *Aliened American*, *Frederick Douglass' Paper*, and the *Liberator*. Since these newspapers and journals were nationally distributed, Harper's inspired works soon earned her a national reputation as a talented poet.

While her move to Philadelphia had stimulated her growth, intellectually and creatively, Harper had not yet realized her dream to become an agent for the Underground Railroad. In the continuing search for the realization of this goal, Harper left Philadelphia and moved to the 'hot-bed' of the fugitives and the anti-slavery movement: New Bedford, Massachusetts. In August 1854, Harper real-ized one of her goals when she was hired as a traveling lecturer by the Maine

Anti-Slavery Society—the first Black woman to be so employed. As such, Harper confronted, on a daily basis, the complex and confusing nineteenth century ideology of gender. During the mid nineteenth century, professional women orators were "rare and highly suspect." "Women who spoke in public to mixed audiences were considered by most people to lack good sense and high moral character."[279] Moreover, while Harper's extensive classical education—with its emphasis on biblical studies, elocution and political leadership—were assets that left her better prepared than most *men* for an oratory career, Frances Foster identifies three personal facets of Harper's life that served to undermine her authority in the eyes of her peers and her audience: youth, marital status, and race.

In philosophical and tangible ways, Harper's chosen profession was a daily assault on nineteenth century ideals of race, gender and class. As a young woman barely thirty years old Harper, by nineteenth century gender standards, was neither a blushing maid nor a mature woman; "Too young to claim the wisdom conceded to women past the childbearing years, but well past the stage when being outspoken was attributed to girlish impulsiveness."[280] As a young unmarried woman Harper had flouted one of the tenets of true womanhood by not achieving, and seemingly not *caring* to achieve, the supposedly coveted title of wife. Since marriage was purportedly the only and overriding proper goal of a young woman's life, "Failure to marry was synonymous with failure in life."[281] In addition, according to nineteenth century gender ideology, true ladies were discreet, quiet and unassuming. They rarely spoke in a public setting and *never* to an audience that included men. Thus, Harper's chosen profession left her vulnerable to "censure as both a failed and a fallen woman."[282] As a young unmarried woman who was also Black, Harper's stance behind a lectern broke yet another unwritten rule of gender and race relations in antebellum America. A pathetic irony of the abolitionist movement was that although its white members were morally opposed enough to the institution of slavery to risk their well-beings to bring about its downfall, the majority of them were also racist; and abolitionist groups were overwhelmingly segregated.

Yet Harper had set her course and had the personal ambition and drive to match. From 5 September to 20 October 1854, Harper launched an impressive schedule on the antislavery lecture circuit—giving thirty-three lectures in twenty-one New England villages and cities. When orating before and audience that could number several hundred, Harper eloquently and passionately laid bare the reality of the true nature of slavery and the unrelenting resolve, by free and enslaved African Americans alike, to win their freedom and their own coveted slice of the American Dream: "…when the restless yearnings for liberty shall burn through the heart and brain—when, tortured by wrong and goaded by oppression, the hearts that would madden with misery, or break in despair, resolve to break their thrall, and escape from bondage, then let the bay of the bloodhound and the scent of the human tiger be upon their track…shall we not hope, that the mental and moral aspect which we present is but the first step of a mighty advancement, the faintest coruscations of the day that will dawn with unclouded splendor upon our downtrodden and benighted race, and that ere long we may present to the admiring gaze of those who wish us well, a people to whom knowledge had given power, and righteousness exaltation?"[283] While her peers and audience may have first viewed Harper's presence with trepidation, her undeniable talent and eloquence soon made her a popular and sought after lecturer.

Harper was not only breaking new ground on the speaker's platform but in the forging of interracial relations as well. Being the first, and at that time the only, Black woman employed by an antislavery society meant that Harper would always travel and lodge with her white female counterparts and Harper was keenly attuned to the unique nature and social significance of such an arrangement: "The agent of the State Anti-Slavery Society of Maine travels with me, and she is a pleasant, dear, sweet lady. I do like her so. We travel together, eat together, and sleep together…but I have a pleasant time. My life reminds me of a beautiful dream…I have met with some of the kindest treatment that I have ever received…"[284] Harper's unconventional career choice gave her the freedom to personally move from theory to practice and act upon her philosophy on successful interracial relations.

Harper's abolitionist career is a prime example of the complex and seemingly contradictory nature of Black Victorian Feminism. On the one hand, she viewed herself, and was largely viewed by others (in the Black community and the larger society) as a confirmed and loyal member of true womanhood. In her written works as well as from behind the lectern, Harper's language was 'chaste' and her literature 'moral.' Reports of her were rife with description of her dignified and composed 'slender and graceful form' and her 'soft musical voice.'[285] On the other hand, while Harper was a Lady in every way, as an orator and writer "her arguments [were] forcible…her logic fervent, her imagination fervid, and her delivery original and easy."[286] Moreover, Harper firmly believed that it would take more than moral suasion to abolish slavery. One manner of protest and resistance that Harper was a staunch supporter of and herself employed was Free Produce: "I believe in that kind of Abolition. Oh, it does seem to strike at one of the principal roots of the matter…slavery fattens and feasts upon human blood…how can we pamper our appetites upon luxuries drawn from reluctant fingers? Oh, could slavery exist long if it did not sit on a commercial throne?"[287]

Not content to solely utilize the pen and platform for the antislavery cause, Harper regularly collected donations that always included some of her own meager salary. Yes, Harper viewed and carried herself as a Lady but she also unhesitatingly drew upon other aspects of her Black womanhood. In April 1858 Harper was unceremoniously 'reminded' of how, around any corner at any given time, racism could and would rear its ugly head. While riding a Philadelphia city railcar a conductor approached Harper and demanded that she exit the car. "Now, was that not brave and noble? As a matter of course I did not."[288] Before the incident escalated further, a white rider intervened and asked the conductor to allow Harper to sit in a corner. But Harper had no intention of moving to the platform or a corner. "I did not move, but kept the same seat. When I was about to leave, he refused my money, and I threw it down on the car floor, and got out, after I had ridden as far as I wished. Such impudence!"[289]

But Harper was not finished. At the first opportunity Harper *published* a detailed account of the incident in the *Liberator*. Harper's letter, in this case, is priceless because it provides a pointed example of how Black Victorian Feminists viewed their own womanhood and how, through their confrontation of the larger society's gender ideology, they were able to assert that this ideology was fatally flawed. By ironically commenting on the conductor's 'brave and noble' act in attempting to remove her from the car, Harper reified how 'ungentlemanly' the conductor's actions were. For whether he believed Harper to be a Lady or no, no true gentleman would ever act so unchivalrously—according to nineteenth century gender ideology. Moreover, Harper affirmed her 'Lady's worth' by refusing the conductor the right to deny or ignore her true womanhood. Thus, in action and attitude, cloaked in the decorum and social graces of her Black womanhood, Harper flexed the muscles of her displeasure, asserted and confirmed the validity of her true womanhood, proved the fallacy of the larger society's gender ideology, and then *published it for all the world and posterity to see*. Harper's professional and literary success, however, came at a high personal cost.

Life for a Black abolitionist activist was dangerous and difficult. The Fugitive Slave Act, in particular, represented two ever-present threats to Harper's life and well being. First, as an activist she would be imprisoned if caught aiding and abetting fugitive slaves. Second, as a *Black* activist, there was the equally ever present threat of being fallaciously enslaved at anytime and in anyplace. In addition, Harper was engaged in the seemingly never-ending personal and professional battle against racism and sexism within and without the abolitionist movement. "On the Carlisle road, I was interrupted and insulted several times. Two men came after me in one day…the shadow of slavery, oh, how drearily it hangs!"[290] But Harper remained undaunted and resolute in her ultimate goal: "If the liberation of the slave demanded it, I would consent to part with a portion of the blood from my own veins if that would do him any good."[291]

Nevertheless, for a time, Harper seriously considered retiring from active involvement in the antislavery crusade, but not because of the dangers and difficulties of her profession, but for her personal health. Years of traveling and lecturing had taken their toll "…the doctor thinks my lungs are weak, and that I need rest more than medicine. That rest may soon be the unbroken slumber of the grave."[292] Yet even with the prospect of being forced to leave her profession due to serious health problems and fatigue, Harper's concern was not with herself but with the plight of enslaved African Americans: "Should I not be permitted to labor much longer, will you not remember my poor blighted and crushed people, and do what you can for them?"[293] Eventually Harper's health improved and she decided to continue her antislavery crusade. One pressing reason was financial in nature. Harper was a young, single Black woman who had the rare opportunity to be entirely self-sufficient. To put it bluntly, she needed the money. More importantly, Harper had committed her life's energies to ending the greatest obstacle facing each and every African American—slavery. And the political and cultural battle over the Slaveocracy was unarguably the most important issue of the antebellum era. Keenly aware of this, for Harper participation in the antislavery movement was a crucial endeavor that emanated from a higher calling: "Oh, life is fading away, and we have but an hour of time! Should we not, therefore, endeavor to let its history gladden the earth? The nearer we ally ourselves to the wants and woes of humanity in the spirit of Christ, the closer we get to the great heart of God; the nearer we stand by the beating pulse of universal love."[294]

Fannie Barrier Williams is perhaps the most unconventional of these seven Black Ladies when considered from a Black Feminist or even Black Victorian Feminist viewpoint. She was not only the second or third generation in her family to be born free, her formative years were spent in a respected free Northern, educated and prosperous, upper-middle-class Black family in an all white town. As such her intellectual and social beliefs had a flavor quite distinct from that of her six contemporaries. Williams' personal and public intellectual and social beliefs and activism, for example, partly emerged from her views on the nature of Black multiracial identity. The majority of nineteenth century Americans (Black and white) believed that a person with even one African ancestor was a 'Negro.' Williams, however, viewed the nature of Black ancestry as much more complex.

Although she herself used the term Negro, Williams was quick to point out that as a descriptive term Negro was wholly inadequate: "The chief objection urged against the term Negro is that it is not ethnically descriptive when applied to hundreds of thousands of people...A mulatto, a quadroon, an octoroon, or a creole, is not a Negro except by a false classification, based upon the common condition of an inferior status."[295] Thus, according to Williams, the term failed to indicate, in form and content, the dizzying varieties that made up the Black community. Instead Williams suggested that the term 'colored,' although lacking in precision and ethnic meaning, was more favorable because it lacked the connotations of hatred, contempt and disrespect that was unfortunately and unavoidable attendant to the term Negro. Williams believed that the term/name 'colored' was worlds away from the baggage entailed in Negro that was often slandered into the term nigger. Moreover, as the Black community continued the inevitable progressive journey toward acquisition of full citizenship rights and recognition, Williams believed the term colored would eventually fade away as a term denoting racial hierarchical difference and be used in the American lexicon as a 'mere term of convenience,' on par with the descriptive term of brunette, for example: "When it is remembered that the so-called Negro race, or colored race, is in language, religion, and instinct as thoroughly American as any of the other races who have come to America and lost their race identity, there is no reason why...they should be known and designated as anything else than Americans."[296] Williams' views on Black ancestry is one characterization of how she refused to dichotomize her Black conscience and Black activism. Another is the stance she took on one of the most important issues concerning the nineteenth century Black community—industrial versus classical education.

By the turn-of-the-century, segregation, disfranchisement, 'Lynch Law,' and a myriad of legal and societal indignities had urged the fledgling Black community to devise and implement its own strategies of social, cultural and economic advancement. During the Slaveocracy the free Black community in the North, the future foundation of the post-Slaveocratic Black community, pooled their resources and utilized cooperative action to establish and build Black organizations and institutions. Especially schools. During the Slaveocracy the main concern was the establishment of an educational institution. By the turn-of-the-century, however, leaders in the Black community were not debating the importance of education, but which form of education would best afford African Americans the opportunity to realize the advancement of their community.

There were two schools of thought vying for predominance in the Black educational curriculum: industrial and classical. Industrial (or vocational training) advocates contended that since the vast majority of African Americans were engaged in a life and death struggle to survive, vocational training offered a tangible means to secure an economically viable livelihood. Thus "...top priority should be given to acquiring skills to earn a living; not even the loss of the right to vote mattered."[297] Proponents of industrial centered education believed that once the Black community had a firm economic foothold, then 'more ambitious goals could be considered,' They were concerned with the Black community as a whole, not the aspirations of the individual. Furthermore, while they did not *theoretically* oppose classical educational for African Americans, neither African Americans nor the larger society were yet ready for a Black classical curriculum.

Advocates of a classical curriculum in Black schools believed that provision of an extensive liberal arts education would be, in the long run, essential to the advancement of the Black community. It would prepare those students who excelled—the 'Talented Tenth'—for higher education and the opportunity to become the next generation of community teachers, leaders and institution builders. Classical education advocates supported industrial educational, theoretically and *practically*. But they were also strongly opposed to the *supplanting* of a classical curriculum by an industrial program that was touted to be more 'realistic' and 'appropriate' for African Americans—such terms implied the innate inferiority of the Black mind and intellectual ability. Classical educational advocates contended that "...the choice between alternative types of education was an individual matter; the criterion must be *aptitude*, not race."[298]

The debate over industrial versus classical education polarized the Black community. Williams' involvement in this debate, however, presented a third viewpoint that suggested that the two schools of thought were not necessarily mutually exclusive. On the contrary, she insisted the industrial 'arts' as well as the classical arts offered rich opportunities for nineteenth century Black women.

"The kind of stupidity that calls industrial education drudgery is the same kind of stupidity that looks upon the kitchen as a place for drudges."[299] Williams, herself a member of the 'Talented Tenth,' believed in and defended the necessity and importance of a classical educational curriculum for all African Americans. Yet she was also vividly aware of the fact that the vast majority of nineteenth century African Americans were poor and often illiterate. The either/or sentiment that characterized the polarized factions in the industrial/classical debate oversimplified, in Williams' view, this large, complex situation that the Black community was grappling with. Williams, on the other hand, offered a sophisticated and radical strategy that accommodated both schools of thought and offered an ingenious way for empowering African Americans not only to economically survive, but also to find/build a viable route from which to transcend economically.

In consideration of the raging debate and the nineteenth century Black woman, Williams was sure of two things: first, "The field for [the Black woman's] skill, her endurance, her finer instincts and faithfulness is ever enlarging; and she has become impatient of limitations…"[300] Second, industrial education (and by natural extension, employment) offered a vast as yet untapped resource that could empower Black women to transcend and eventually obliterate the limitations forced upon them by the larger society. Williams contended that it was a waste of energy and soul to 'fret' over the lack of broader educational and occupational opportunity. Instead, she urged those Black women who chose or had to work menial jobs to face that reality and manipulate it to their benefit: "What, then, shall we do for the young woman with refined instincts and fair education? She is ambitious to choose and follow the occupation for which she is best fitted by talents and inclination, but she is shut out from most employments open to other women, and does not realize that her refinement and training are as much needed and as well paid for in domestic service as in other occupations."[301] Williams' strategy for transforming domestic service from a limited occupational sphere to a springboard from which Black women could further elevate themselves and their womanhood was two-fold: to change the understandably negative Black perception of domestic service and to professionalize domestic service.

Williams contended that domestic service in itself was not necessarily degrading. What understandably made it a degrading occupation for Black women was the fact that the vast majority of domestic employers (primarily white housewives) were 'petty tyrants' who believed that domestic servants were "inferior and servile by nature, and must receive treatment accorded to inferiors. [Thus the Black woman] who understands this haughtiness of spirit and exaggerated superiority is always resentful and on the defensive."[302] Williams believed that employers would become more respectful to the Black women upon whom they were dependent 'every hour of the day for case and comfort, health and happiness' once Black women had economic might that equaled the myriad of invaluable services they rendered. And, according to Williams, there was only one way that might would be realized—professionalization of domestic service.

Williams, too, held the Black community responsible for the derogatory reputation of domestic service: "If our girls work for wages in a nice home, rather than in a factory or over a counter, they are ruthlessly scorned by their friends and acquaintances…The every-day [Black] man and woman who make society must change their foolish notions as to what is the polite thing for a young woman to do."[303] Whether the Black community liked it or not, wanted it to be or not to be, the majority of employed Black women, educated and uneducated, worked as domestics. These women were substantial financial contributors to their households. These women, through their donations and service, were the backbone of the Black community's strongest institutions (i.e. the Church and schools). These women had earned and deserved respect, not only from the larger society that oppressed them all, but from their own community as well.

The other and more important reason, in Williams' opinion, that domestic service was not a degrading occupation was that the high degree of personal character, intelligence and competency a Black woman brought to her workplace meant that she could never be a servant in the derogatory sense of the word. In addition, domestic service, as an occupation in itself, had in it "the elements of high art and much science. It is an occupation that intelligence elevates, the character adorns and ennobles, and that even now brings a higher salary to women than most any other kind of employment."[304] Nevertheless, Williams insisted that until domestic service became a recognized and respected profession (by both the white and Black communities) Black women would remain largely unable to reap the largely ignored potential benefits of domestic service. Thus, Williams called for the establishment of schools of 'domestic science,' where training for this new profession would be elevated "to the dignity and importance of the training in mathematics and grammar and other academic studies."[305]

Yes, the triad of oppression imposed harsh limitations on the educational and career aspirations of Black women. Williams believed that in tandem with Black women's efforts to eradicate these artificial limitations they should empower themselves to tap the unrealized power and advantages of, in this case domestic service, and transform existing opportunities into fresh *profitable* opportunity. She cited that in her home city of Chicago, for example, domestic service was the sole occupation in which the demand for Black women exceeded the supply. Thus, two important factors could be counted as advantageous for the Black women who freely, or through economic necessity, chose a domestic career: "…the wages paid are higher than those given for the same grade of intelligence in any other calling, and that colored women can command almost a monopoly of this employment."[306] Williams urged Black women to exploit this circumstance to their own benefit. While she did not advocate the restriction of Black women to industrial education and domestic service, Williams believed that Black women were ignoring the great economic opportunity represented by industrial education and a professionalized domestic service career: "Shall we lead or shall we follow this movement? Shall we, in this as in many other things, beg for an opportunity further on instead of helping to create opportunities now?"[307]

Fannie Barrier Williams is appropriately illustrative of the complex and intricate nature of Black Victorian Feminism. Her personal views and 'public' activism were the result of an at times uneasy mixture of Victorian middle class ideals on gender, race and class, and the everyday reality of nineteenth century African American women's lives. Williams was in the rare position of being a nineteenth century educated upper-middle-class Black woman. Her social position empowered her with intimate knowledge of and interaction with the larger society. Her Blackness and 'womaness' empowered her with intimate knowledge of the realities of nineteenth century Black women's lives, regardless of class position. Her education and experience empowered her to speak and act out against racism and sexism with and through an intellectually and politically engaged voice. Williams' stance on industrial versus classical education and employment for African American women provides fertile ground from which to explore this fascinating woman's Black Victorian Feminist discourse and intellectual enterprise.

Seventy Tumultuous Years...

Through all the blight of slavery they kept their womanhood, and now they march with heads erect, to fight for all things good, nor care for scorn nor seek praise, just so they please their God.

—Clara Ann Thompson, dedication from *Homespun Heroines*

These seven women's lives encompassed seventy years of a tumultuous time in Black history: the Slaveocracy, the Civil War, Reconstruction and Jim/Jane Crow (dejure in the South and defacto in the North). During that time African Americans formed a psychic and physical community, enslaved and free—in part to negotiate amidst a larger society determined to oppress them and in part to realize an individual and collective desire to achieve social, political and economic prosperity. During and immediately after the Slaveocracy these women, with their families or on their own, joined the Black migration north in search of their piece of the American Dream. But they brought with them their individual and collective life experiences. In many ways, with the exception of Fannie Barrier Williams, these women's stories are similar to the tens of thousands of stories of nineteenth century Black women, how they gained their freedom, headed north seeking a better and brighter future, rolled up their sleeves and joined Black men in the backbreaking and dangerous endeavor to build a Black community with strong institutions.

Again with the exception of Williams, these 'Ladies' were either born enslaved or were the children of slaves. The majority of them achieved their freedom when a Black parent or loved one worked and saved enough money to purchase the freedom of their loved ones. They were all directly related to the white person who owned them and/or their parents. They all worked full-time jobs to support themselves and contribute to their families' income and they were all able to achieve a modicum of financial security, though they worked their entire lives to ensure that security. Nevertheless, there are several interrelated factors unique to these seven women's lives that empowered them to move themselves from being women just trying to survive to women destined to transcend and be able to act on an unshakable belief in the existence and redemptive power of Black womanhood and in the process to take radical and libratory action to bring about revolutionary change. The Brown, Cooper, Coppin, Early, Harper, Wells and Williams stories may be similar to the stories of many nineteenth century Black women, but there are some factors unique to these seven women's lives that enabled them to don the mantle of Black Victorian Feminism: education, self-sufficiency and an understanding of how the trope of gender and race crucially informed their lives and their activism.

A common trait shared by these women, that was an extremely rare trait for the vast majority of nineteenth century Black women, was their possession of an extensive education. Within the Black community education was touted as one of the primary mechanisms of racial uplift. Black Victorian Feminists emphasized "...the importance of building an intellectual and professional elite, calling upon the 'leading' or 'intelligent' or 'better class' of Negroes to take initiative for their people."[308] Brown, Cooper, Coppin and Early earned college degrees; Harper attended a prestigious academy for Black children; Wells supplemented her educational acumen in a literary society; and Williams attended several schools, including a prestigious music conservatory, after graduating from State Normal school.

Another common and rare trait shared by these women was their ability to successfully financially support themselves in conventional and unconventional ways. One conventional position shared by all of them was the teaching profession. Education and academic achievement in general, the teaching profession in particular, offered a route to economic freedom and a good measure of economic security. To be sure, the life of a teacher was full of challenges: "...crude school facilities, the poverty of their students, the shortened school year, and white hostility...[and] an inequitable pay scale..."[309] Yet there were tangible advantages as well. Although the pay scale and facilities fell far short of what their white counterparts enjoyed, Black women teachers earned more than agricultural workers or domestics. Moreover, inherent in the teaching profession was a social and political activist ethic. In very real ways teaching African Americans to read and write, providing a space for Black people to intellectualize their experience and the world in which they lived represented a daily form of effective resistance to oppression and demoralization.

Black teachers were members of a network of educators and builders of institutions. Some of them were published (all of these 'Ladies' were), traveled extensively, and participated in a large variety of public events (i.e. the World's Congress of Representative Women). African American women teachers were recognized as leaders in and of the Black community; and that community gave them respect and recognition. Therefore, not only did the teaching profession provide a route to middle class status and economic stability, it empowered its practitioners with a sense of individual self-worth and a collective pride for the crucial part they played in the endeavor of racial uplift and the elevation of Black womanhood. By the late nineteenth century not only was academic achievement believed to be a vital element for the advancement of the Black community, Black Victorian Feminists espoused the belief that academic achievement was essential for the molding of the ideal woman. Through academic achievement and participation in the teaching profession Black Victorian Feminists believed that they and all Black women would be representative of the intelligence, morality and resourcefulness characteristic of the entire African American community. Essential to these seven 'Ladies' accomplishments was their ability to financially support themselves. While Brown, Early and Williams had privileged, or relatively privileged, upbringings, Cooper, Coppin, Harper and Wells began supporting themselves as adolescents or teenagers. Through their determination and ambition, they were all able to provide themselves the precious time and space necessary to better themselves and agitate for the uplift of their community and the elevation of Black womanhood. Another trait unique to these seven women was the unconventional ways they financially supported and simultaneously expressed themselves.

In summation, Brown, Cooper, Coppin, Early, Harper, Williams and Wells are representative examples of Black Victorian Feminist theory and methodology. While their individual voices were unique there are, nevertheless, several common traits to be found in their work. As a group, and individually, these seven 'Ladies' were committed to the power of education; the eradication of illiteracy, employment barriers, racial and gender discrimination. To this end they each offered deft and complex analyses from an intellectualized and politicized nineteenth century Black woman's standpoint. Their work, in whatever vehicle of expression they utilized, reified the interaction between race and power, and the interaction between gender and power. This analysis was structured by a keen awareness of history (Black and white), ideology (Black and white), available material resources (or the lack thereof), and an ideology of respectability and emotion. These women—in their words and actions—refused to dichotomize their loyalties. They could and did work with, through and around a myriad of social issues that affected the Black community and the larger society. For them community uplift and the elevation of Black womanhood were related endeavors; thus they acknowledged no conflict in dedicating their efforts to both. Finally, the primary constant in their lives and activism was their endeavor to render the African American woman visible to the Black community and the larger society, 'capitalized and personified.' At every opportunity they reified the importance of Black women's work (within and without the Black community). They gave the nineteenth century Black woman voice, shape and substance and worked to empower her to render herself visible, heard. It is no wonder that they met, in a forum ostensibly assembled to discuss the importance of women's work and women's lives, at the Columbian Exposition.

4

I AM THE UTTERANCE OF MY NAME

I am the first and the last.
I am the honored one and the scorned one.
I am the whore and the holy one.
I am the wife and the virgin.
I am the barren one and many are my daughters.
I am the silence that you cannot understand.
I am the utterance of my name.

—Julie Dash, *Daughters of the Dust*

Setting the Scene: The Columbian Exposition of 1893

"We are met this day to honor the memory of Christopher Columbus [we] bid you partake with us these fruits of four hundred years of American civilization and development and behold these trophies of one hundred years of American independence and freedom."[310] On June 5, 1890, through an act of Congress, President Benjamin Harrison had created a National Commission to oversee the planning and implementation of a world's fair—the Columbian Exposition—to be held in Chicago, Illinois in 1893. The explicitly stated purpose of this world's fair was to present to the world that the United States represented the pinnacle of modern civilization; and this predominance would be showcased in a 'White City'—that consisted of fifteen main buildings, housing exhibits of the latest technological and agricultural innovations, and artistic and intellectual production. Naturally, African Americans—who had successfully built and fortified a community and institutions only twenty-eight years removed from slavery and

92

under to most dire of circumstances—viewed the Exposition as the perfect opportunity for national and international representation and recognition.

Black community leaders sought, nay *demanded*, full participation in the decision making and planning of the fair. In addition, they sought the installation of a separate exhibit of, for and about African Americans in the White City: "They based their claim to representation as a distinct group on more than two centuries of unrewarded toil along with an unwavering loyalty to the highest ideals of the nation."[311] They soon realized, however, that while 'all nations and creeds be welcome here,' African Americans were not.[312] One Democrat and one Republican from every state and territory, nominated by state and territorial governers and selected by President Harrison, were appointed to the National Commission. No African American, male or female, was appointed to this commission. Undaunted, African American community leaders took their fight for inclusion to Washington, where they first submitted applications for the appointment of a Black representative to George R. Davis—the Director General of the management affairs department of the Exposition: "The Director General declined to make any such appointment."[313] Next, they approached the fair's National Directors and petitioned for the establishment of a Department of Colored Exhibits in the Exposition: "This suggestion was considered by the National Directors and it was decided that no separate exhibit for colored people be permitted."[314]

Despite their Herculean efforts Black community leaders were only able to garner the appointment of one Black man as an alternate member of the National Commission. Recognizing that the National Commission would never accept an African American within its ranks, Black community leaders hoped that "...in the work undertaken by the women there would be sympathy and a helpful influence for colored women."[315] On April 25, 1890, Congress approved a Board of Lady Managers, selected by President Harrison. This Board was comprised of 117 members, two from each state and territory, and the District of Columbia. The purpose of the Board of Lady managers was to collect and display 'exhibits' of American women from all over the nation in a Woman's Building, serving as a monument to the important role that women had played in the advancement of civilization.

Three days before the first meeting of the Board of Lady Managers, a 'Ladies mass-meeting' convened at the Bethesda Baptist Chapel in Chicago, Illinois. The purpose of this meeting was to discuss the manner in which the progress and achievements of African American women would be presented at the Exposition in general, the Woman's Building in particular. On 25 November 1890, The Women's Columbian Association formally presented their petition to the Board:

> WHEREAS no provisions have, as yet, been made by the World's Columbian Exposition Commission for securing exhibits from the colored women of this country, or the giving of representation to them in such Fair, and WHEREAS under the present arrangement and classification of exhibits, it would be impossible for visitors to the Exposition to know and distinguish the exhibits and handwork of the colored women from those of the Anglo-Saxons, and because of this the honor, fame and credit for all meritorious exhibits, though made by some of our race, would not be duly given us, therefore be it RESOLVED, that for the purpose of demonstrating the progress of the colored women since emancipation and of showing to those who are yet doubters, and there are many, that the colored women have [made] and are making rapid strides in art, science, and manufacturing, and of furnishing to all information as to the educational and industrial achievement made by the race, and what the race has done, is doing, and might do, in every department of life, that we, the colored women of Chicago request the World's Columbian Commission to establish an office for a colored woman whose duty it shall be to collect exhibits from the colored women of America…[316]

The Women's Columbian Association (W.C.A.) petitioned the Board of Lady Managers for the appointment of an African American woman to the Board, who would organize a separate (segregated) exhibit that would demonstrate African American women's progress and achievement since emancipation. Soon thereafter, another organization of Black women, the Women's Columbian Auxiliary Association (W.C.A.A.), petitioned the Board for the appointment of an African American woman to the Board who would collect and organize an inclusive (integrated) exhibit. Furthermore, this appointee would also participate in the policy-making decisions of the Board. Finally, the W.C.A.A. sought the employment of African American women in administrative and clerical positions at the Women's Headquarters on the fairgrounds.

Thus, a procedural rift appeared amid Black Victorian Feminists over the best avenue for Black women's representation at the Exposition. On the one hand, the camp represented by the W.C.A.A. was against a segregated exhibit on the grounds that African American women were "…American citizens and desire[d] to draw no line that would tend to make us strangers in the land of our birth."[317] On the other hand, the camp represented by the W.C.A. felt that a segregated Black women's exhibit offered greater visibility amid thousands of other exhibits. Nevertheless, Black Victorian Feminists were united in their overarching goal—the wholesale inclusion of African American women in "...this international event of monumental importance."[318] Black Victorian Feminists laid claim to the right of representation as a distinct group, as a matter of racial entitlement, entitlement born of centuries of enslavement coupled with staunch loyalty by African Americans to the highest American ideals. Entitlement was further solidified by twenty-eight years of truly incredible progress and achievement by African American women since emancipation.

Blindsided by and unprepared to deal with this unexpected and vocal challenge to her authority, Bertha Palmer (the President of the Board of Lady Managers) latched onto the 'procedural rift' amid the Black Victorian Feminist petitioners "...the Board of Lady Managers eagerly availed itself of the opportunity to say that the colored people were divided into factions and it would be impolite to recognize either faction."[319] In the end, the Board of Lady Managers proposed that all Black women's petitions be referred to the various separate state boards compiling state exhibits that would then be sent to the Exposition. Undaunted, the W.C.A. and the W.C.A.A. decided to take their fight to Washington, D.C. The first national African American women's conference would be held to lobby for the wholesale inclusion of Black women's contributions to American civilization. In preparation for this event, a circular was sent out, nationwide, calling on "...the representative Negro women of the United States, urging them to meet...[on] October 21, 1891, to take steps relating to the Negro woman's interest in the world's Columbian exposition and earnestly solicited a number of representative colored women to be present to lend their assistance in this great and important movement."[320] Unfortunately, the first national Black women's conference failed to garner the unified political and social support needed to organize a Black women's exhibit, segregated or integrated, for the Exposition. Several prominent Black women, however, answered the nationwide call for 'representative colored women.' Hallie Quinn Brown, Anna Julia Cooper, Fanny Jackson Coppin, Sarah Jane Early and Frances Ellen Watkins Harper were among the eleven chosen as possible representative delegates to the Exposition. At about this time Ida B. Wells decided to compose, and elicit the literary contributions of several Black intellectuals for a protest pamphlet to be distributed at the fair: "The pamphlet is intended as a calm, dignified statement of the Afro-American's side of the story...a statement of the fruitless efforts he has made for representation at the world's fair."[321]

Ida B. Wells did not attend, nor participate in, the *World's Congress of Representative Women.* Mrs. Isabelle Fyvie Mayo, a Scottish author and civil rights activist, invited Wells to Aberdeen, Scotland to speak about the results of her research of 'lynch law' in America, which began Wells' worldwide campaign against lynching. From April to May 1893, Wells traveled throughout Scotland and England lecturing about America's lynch law. But before Wells received Mayo's invitation, she had joined forces with Frederick Douglass in raising funds for the publication of the informational pamphlet to be distributed at the Exposition. Unfortunately, her commitments in Europe and at the Exposition overlapped. While Wells was unable to attend the World's Congress of Representative Women she did spend the last three months of the Exposition passing out ten thousand copies of her pamphlet. Entitled *The Reason Why the Colored American Is Not in the World's Columbian Exposition*, the booklet was "…a clear, plain statement of facts concerning the oppression put upon the colored people in this land of the free and home of the brave."[322]

Wells's pamphlet explained that in May 1893 the African American population of eight million constituted one out of every ten American citizens. African Americans contributed greatly to the country's prosperity and civilization. African Americans were half of the country's work-force, a work-force that afforded the larger white population the 'space,' time and opportunity essential to the country's successful progress in education, art, science, industry, and invention—everything that was being celebrated at the Exposition. This being the case, why weren't African Americans represented at the Exposition's 'White City' and Midway Plaisance? "It is to answer these questions and supply as far as possible our lack of representation at the Exposition that the African American has published this volume."[323] To those who sought after the truth, Wells and her compatriots offered a painstakingly honest and learned view into the nineteenth century Black experience. Frederick Douglass authored the first chapter of the pamphlet, the introduction. Like Wells and many others, Douglass felt that the glaring absence of representation of African American contribution to education, art, science, industry and invention, to American prosperity and civilization, had to be explored and discussed. For Douglass the answer to why the Black experience and voice had been largely excluded from the Exposition was painfully clear—slavery.

The spirit of that cruel and degrading institution that had, for nearly three hundred years, perverted personal and national moral perception, conscience, character, religious teaching and common sense had perverted the noble sentiment and purpose of the Exposition too. Douglass contended that a powerful element in the larger society was 'uncomfortable' with the incredible progress (educationally, economically, socially, and culturally) that African Americans had attained, thus a concerted effort was being made to stunt this growth—and the exclusion of Black people from participating in the Exposition was one manifestation of this impulse. Nevertheless, in spite of the larger society's often brutal attempts to bring about the contrary, "there is no stopping any people from earnestly endeavoring to rise."[324] In conclusion, Douglass encouraged all African Americans to continue to become more than even they thought that they could be for "Next to victory is the glory and happiness of manfully contending for it. Therefore, contend! contend! Conflict is better than stagnation. It is bad to be a slave, but worse to be a willing and contented slave..."[325]

In the second chapter, entitled "Class Legislation," Ida B. Wells explored the genesis of segregation, also known as 'Jim/Jane Crow'. Wells' detailed the de jure and de facto means by which the larger society began to systematically oppress African Americans. Chapters Three and Four, also by Wells, discussed at length two particularly brutal mechanisms of Black oppression. The first mechanism was the Convict Lease System wherein "[a state government]...claim[s] to be too poor to maintain state convicts within prison walls. Hence the convicts are leased out to work for railway contractors, mining companies, and those who farm large plantations. These companies...work them as cheap labor and pay the states handsome revenue for their labor. Nine-tenths of these convicts are Negros". The second brutal mechanism of Black oppression was the theme of Chapter Four: 'Lynch Law.' In both cases Wells noted how the American legal and judicial systems are the primary conduit for the continuity of these forms of Black oppression. Entitled, 'The Progress of the Afro-American Since Emancipation," Chapter Five, by I. Garland Penn, is a detailed statistical analysis of Black achievement in education, the professions, literature, journalism, the church, business interests (i.e. personal wealth and property ownership), music, poetry, the trades and manual labor, and an extensive listing of patents "...granted by the United States for inventions by colored persons."[326] The final chapter, "The Reason Why" by F.L. Barnett, is a moment to moment account of how African Americans were excluded from the Exposition and how African Americans valiantly, and unsuccessfully, fought for the right of inclusion, representation, and recognition.

The Reason Why the Colored American Is Not in the World's Columbian Exposition brilliantly accomplished its purpose. It provided the nation and the world a concise summary of "...all the things that blacks had done right, as manifested by their accomplishments since emancipation; it exposed things done wrong by whites against African Americans...It also explained what they perceived as their systematic exclusion at the fair for the understanding of the liberal Western white world."[327] But did *The Reason Why* provide a comprehensive picture of Black experience at the Exposition? The pamphlet left the reader with the impression that elements of the larger society had been successful in the attempt to completely exclude African American presence and participation at the Exposition. Indeed in her autobiography, Ida B. Wells lists Frederick Douglass's post as the representative of the Republic of Haiti, at the Haitian Building, as the *only* official Black representation present: "Had it not been for this, Negros of the United States would have had no part nor lot in any official way in the World's Fair. For the United States government had refused her Negro citizens participation therein."[328]

Wells and her cohorts operated from what Christopher Reed had named a 'paradigm emphasizing conflict or protest'. This paradigm places primacy on the dynamic of conflict or protest as an essential component of racial progress. Furthermore, this paradigm relies on a binary approach that constructs, in this case, Black experience at the Exposition as either totally inclusionary or exclusionary. Thus "…the lack of administrative representation at the highest levels of governance at the fair along with the absence of a visual representation of African American achievement through a Negro exhibition"[329] effectively obfuscated any other modes of Black participation. Moreover, for Wells, anything short of protest advocacy for the wholesale and uncompromised inclusion of African Americans "…necessarily precluded a great deal of African American thought, behavior and organizational effort that was manifested before and during 1893…"[330] This possibly explains why Wells chose to detail the protest advocacy attempts for Black women's inclusion at the World's Congress of Representative Women by the W.C.A. and the W.C.A.A. but *makes no mention* of Black women's presence and participation at the World's Congress of Representative Women.

A provocative conundrum arises when considering *The Reason Why* as one comprehensive source to gauge the participation of Black women, or the lack their of, at the Exposition. Wells was in England in May 1893—during the World's Congress of Representative Women. She wrote and edited *The Reason Why* during the midpoint of the Exposition and distributed her pamphlet during the last three months of the Exposition (August, September and October 1893). Thus primary or even partial reliance on the pamphlet as an evaluative source is problematic. While *The Reason Why* is "…an exceptional statement of the hopes, the fears, the achievements, the disappointments and, significantly, the…grievances…"[331] of nineteenth century African Americans, it leaves little room for the consideration of an alternate paradigm of racial progress, one that places primacy on continuous resistance and challenge as a measuring tool for gauging the level and success of African American women's presence and participation at the Exposition. The legacy of *The Reason Why*, however, cannot be reduced to a simple exercise of protest advocacy, where racial progress was measured through the prism of conflict and protest. It provides an in depth, highly informative view of the lives of nineteenth century African Americans. Most importantly, Wells pamphlet is a valuable primary source historical document of Black history and Black women's history. While I believe that the contemporary and historical importance of *The Reason Why* is unquestionable, the fact remains that Wells and her compatriots were steadfastly wedded to this either totally inclusionary or totally exclusionary paradigm and approach that they ignored one segment of the Black community that was successful in garnering Black recognition and representation at the Exposition—Black Victorian Feminists.

Where 'organized' efforts for Black women's inclusion had been ineffectual, individual efforts proved to be harder for the Board of Lady Managers to ignore. Hallie Quinn Brown first came onto the 'Exposition scene' via her letter of application to Bertha Palmer's Colored Employment Application Index. Brown's credentials were impressive. She was highly educated, eloquent and possessed the related experience of being the organizer of a Black exhibit at the Southern Interstate Exposition in Raleigh, North Carolina in 1891. In March 1892 Brown traveled to Chicago for an interview with Palmer who was understandably impressed with the young lady. "[Miss Brown is]…intelligent…inclined to be very dramatic and make telling statements…"[332] In the meanwhile, Brown decided to test the validity and effectiveness of the Board's pronouncement that Black women's exhibits be compiled and organized at the state level. She wrote to each individual state Black organization and asked them to confirm if their state ladies managers were assisting in facilitating Black women's representation at the Exposition:

DEAR SIR: Please inform me by letter, or through the columns of your valuable paper, if the colored women or the colored people as a whole in your state and section have been called upon by your state lady managers to form auxiliaries and to organize for active work in the interest of the world's fair to be held in this city in 1893. If not, are they co-operating with any organized body sanctioned by the state lady managers? I share the common interest of the race in how far our women are expected to participate in the Columbian exposition. I adopt this plan to ascertain what influence had been brought to bear and what activity has been awakened throughout the country. An early reply will be appreciated by

Yours sincerely, HALLIE Q. BROWN[333]

The reply to every missive sent was that no action had been taken by individual state lady managers. Next, Brown set a letter of inquiry to each member of the Board of Lady Managers asking for their support in the appointment of a Black woman to oversee the installation of a Black woman's exhibit.

Chicago, Illinois, April 8, 1892
Mrs._____
Lady Manager of the Columbian Exposition for_____

Dear Madam:

It seems to be a settled conviction among the colored people, that no adequate opportunity is to be offered them for proper representation in the World's Fair. A circular recently issued and widely distributed makes that charge direct. That there is an element of truth in it seems apparent, since neither recognition has been granted, nor opportunity offered.

And further it is shown that the intercourse between the two races, particularly in the southern states, is so limited that the interchange of ideas is hardly seriously considered. If, therefore, the object of the Woman's Department of the Columbian Exposition is to present to the world the industrial and educational progress of the bread winners-the wage women-how immeasurably incomplete will that work be without the exhibit of the thousands of the colored women of this country.

The question naturally arises, who is awakening an interest among our colored women, especially in the South where the masses are, and how many auxiliaries have been formed through which they may be advised of the movement that is intended to be so comprehensive and all inclusive? Considering the peculiar relation that the Negro sustains in this country, is it less fair to request for him a special representation?

Presuming that such action would be had, several colored men and women, including the writer, have endorsements of unquestionable strength from all classes of American citizens. These endorsements are on file in the President's office of the Woman's Commission in this city. It is urged at the headquarters that the Lady Managers would seriously object to the appointment of a special representative to canvass the various states. Permit me to emphasize the fact, that this matter is in earnest discussion, among the representatives of eight millions of the population of the United States.

I address this circular to you, kindly requesting your opinion Upon the suggestions made herein, and solicit a reply at your earliest Convenience.

Yours respectfully,
4440 Langley Ave.,
(Miss) Hallie Q. Brown
Chicago, Illinois.[334]

Less than half of the Board responded. At this point agitation for the representation of African American women at the Exposition had reached a fevered pitch. Palmer and the rest of the Board realized that these Ladies were not going away and would not be silent or *silenced*. Palmer offered Brown a position in the Department of Publicity and Promotion. Palmer was of the opinion that Brown could effectively represent the interests of African American women by writing "…for the colored papers, keep in communication with the prominent women of her race; and keep them informed as to what was going on so that they would feel they had 'a friend at court' and were receiving proper attention…"[335] But Brown had other plans. She made it quite clear that she was applying for the self-titled position of 'Solicitor of Exhibits among the Colored People for the Columbian Exposition.' Brown was not interested in Palmer's offer of a 'glorified secretarial position.' She wanted, and demanded, the opportunity to freely collect and organize Black women's exhibits and be a member of the Board of Lady Managers. Palmer decided to ignore and simultaneously squelch the uncomfortable situation. She wrote to Brown: "I asked you to name a salary that you would consider the equivalent of your services and as you have not done so, [I] presume you did not find the position one you cared to fill. Lamenting that this is the case, I certainly cannot blame you, and hoping we may yet find the proper person to take the place."[336] In the end, Brown's aspirations were not realized but she was invited to address the World's Congress of Representative Women.

As a member of Chicago's Black Upper-Middle-Class Social Elite and an active social welfare reformer, Fannie Barrier Williams had uncommon access to the political and upper class social echelons of the larger society. In December 1891 Williams personally contacted a local congressional representative and requested that two African American women be appointed as clerks in the Exposition's Installation Department. The primary purpose of these positions revolved around the acquisition of items for a Black exhibit. After garnering congressional support for her petition, Williams contacted Bertha Palmer, who also agreed to her plan, and Williams petition was adopted. By this point Palmer conceded that a conciliatory gesture on the Board's part was warranted, at the very least, for positive public relations purposes. In January 1893, after Hallie Quinn Brown had rejected the position originally offered by Palmer, Palmer appointed a Black woman—Mrs. A.M. Curtis—to the position of procuring and organizing Black exhibits to be housed in the Woman's Building. Mrs. Curtis soon resigned "…the post was farcical given the few exhibits and the uncooperativeness of the Chief of Installation…"[337] After Curtis' resignation, Palmer appointed Fannie Barrier Williams to aid in the organization of *all* exhibits in the Woman's Building. Williams held the position for seven months, gathering both white and Black exhibits, until the budget was cut and she lost her position. Sadly, a Black woman was not appointed to the Board of Lady Managers and Black women were denied the opportunity to participate in policy making; and the few administrative and clerical positions that were procured were short lived. Yet the Black Victorian Feminist movement for inclusion in and representation did not fail. It was realized in a fabulous manner that subsequently heralded the next phase of Black Feminist history.

In 1892 the directors of the Columbian Exposition elected to hold a formal assembly, a congress, to discuss national and international concerns of the day. Several congresses were formed, focusing on such issues as language, literature, religion, science, art, education, industry, poverty, and domestic life. Women were invited to participate in the congresses, and did, but their participation meant, "…women would appear, not in the role of women, so to speak, but in that of their profession…in company with men belonging to the same professions…pertaining to their respective professions and avocations."[338] The Board of Lady Managers was concerned that such an 'incidental' presence would not fully illustrate that nineteenth-century women had acquired a new conception of self that was not "…harmonious with the former prevailing conception of…[woman] as man's addendum, his helpmeet, his subordinate."[339] Thus, the Board of Lady Managers decided to organize a congress of, by and for women "…in which women might read their own interpretation of their natures, their own version of their rights, responsibilities, duties, and destiny…"[340]

The World's Congress of Representative Women

The desire in woman to tell her own story, to paint her own portrait, to read her own future, a desire so deep that it seemed a duty, so dominating that it amounted to a necessity—made the World's Congress of Representative Women possible.

—May Wright Sewell, *The World's Congress of Representative Women*

A woman's Congress committee, independent of the National Commission and formed under the auspices of the Board of Lady Managers, invited national and international women speakers to address topics of interest to women and to illustrate that "…woman is becoming as capable as man to take her part in this highly centralized and highly specialized civilization."[341] Headed by May Wright Sewall, the Committee for Organization for the World's Congress of Representative Women were looking for "…the most thoughtful, the most finely developed and most highly cultured women [who] considered it important to seize this unique opportunity to present their estimate of woman's place and possibilities."[342] The Committee wanted women who excelled in the fields of education, philanthropic work, religious endeavors, and moral and social reform to participate in the Congress. With this goal in mind, the Committee sent a letter to a 'constituency of twelve hundred' men and women, nationally and internationally, asking for suitable nominations:

> "The Committee of Arrangements desires that this great opportunity shall be used in the way that will further the highest interests of humanity. It therefore is anxious that the programme shall be prepared with the greatest discrimination, and to this end, is asking leaders in the various departments of work, the world over, to aid it by answering the following questions: FIRST. What subjects will you suggest for discussion in the World's Congress of Representative Women? SECOND. What women will you suggest to write papers, or lead in the discussion of the subjects suggested? It must be understood that the committee will find it impossible to place all the subjects and all of the writers presented, in response to the above inquires, upon the programme, but it solicits you to make your lists of both subjects and writers as full as you may desire, and will be very grateful for a prompt response to this appeal."[343]

While Bertha Palmer had been extremely reluctant to aid in the provision of figurative and literal space for African American women on the Board of Lady Managers or in the Woman's Building, Sewall was personally and professionally dedicated to ensuring that every facet of nineteenth century women's voice and experience was represented at the World's Congress of Representative Women: "…we feel it gladder if a humbler duty to unite in it [the World's Congress of Representative Women] the races that are at work together within our own land of liberty. You will find upon our list of speakers…some descendants from that other more outraged race, imported only to be reduced to servitude, who come to us but one remove from the generation of their blood which was sold from the block."[344]

At the first national African American Women's conference in Washington, D.C. a list of representative delegates was compiled and later forwarded to the Committee. Anna Julia Cooper, Fannie Jackson Coppin, Sarah Jane Early and Frances Ellen Watkins Harper were on that list, with good reason.

Anna Julia Cooper was among the first four African American women in the United States to earn a university degree and she had recently published the critically acclaimed *A Voice From the South*. Fannie Jackson Coppin was the second Black woman in the United States to earn a university degree; the first Black woman to occupy the position high school principal; and was a well known and respected social welfare activist in the African American Philadelphia community. Sarah Jane Early had earned a college degree from Oberlin University; was a prominent, well known, and respected activist in the African Methodist Episcopal Church; became the first African American woman on a college faculty when she was appointed Preceptress of English and Latin and Lady Principal and Matron at Wilberforce University (1866); and in 1892 she had been appointed Superintendent of the Colored Division of the Woman's Christian Temperance Union. Frances Ellen Watkins Harper was a well known and respected participant in the Abolitionist movement; was the first Black woman to be employed as a lecturer on the Abolitionist circuit; had published three books of poetry and three novels; and in 1893 she was appointed Superintendent of the Colored Division of the Woman's Christian Temperance Union (after Sarah Jane Early retired from the post). Fannie Barrier Williams first came onto the Exposition scene when she successfully lobbied for an appointment to the Exposition's Installation Department—where, soonthereafter, she occupied the short lived role of organizer of all exhibits for the Woman's Building. Undoubtedly, Williams' cultivation of an amiable relationship with Bertha Palmer, along with her well deserved reputation as a successful Black community builder and leader, resulted in her not only being invited to speak at the World's Congress of Representative Women but also being chosen to serve for one day as Honorary American President of the Congresses and head the panel at the congress of the Solidarity of Human Interests.

The World's Congress of Representative Women ran during the first two weeks of the Columbian Exposition. It featured three hundred and thirty scheduled speakers and more than three hundred unscheduled speakers appearing at seventy-six different sessions. In fact, such a large number of attendees were expected that the directors of the Exposition elected to hold the Women's Congress on a site near the Fairgrounds: the "Art Palace" soon to be the Chicago Art Institute. Women speakers from one hundred and twenty-six organizations represented the countries of Belgium, Brazil, Canada, Denmark, England, Finland, France, Germany, Greece, Ireland, Italy, New South Wales, Norway, Poland, Scotland, South America, Spain, Sweden, Switzerland, and the United States. An estimated audience of 150,000 was in attendance at the Art Palace: "its maximum capacity was taxed by throngs that, filling every room or hall where a meeting was announced, overflowed all these and surged through anterooms and passages, patiently or otherwise waiting the withdrawal of some listener for a chance to obtain standing-place in the always crowded aisles...often hundreds of people were sent away long before the hour of opening a meeting arrived...[thus it] may be inferred the eager desire of the public to hear the views of woman."[345]

These self-proclaimed progressive women wanted to share with each other and the world the fruits of women's intellectual activity, contributions to the evolution of civilization, and their commitment to the procurement of empowering changes for women around the world: "In this Congress all organizations of women whatever name or object, and all distinguished women...will meet on absolutely equal terms for the advancement of the common interests of women everywhere."[346] While the Women's Congress sought to illuminate the accomplishments of all women its greater purpose was to redefine woman's place within the Anglo/andro-American hierarchy and dismantle the more damaging and oppressive aspects of the cult of true white womanhood. These progressive women sought to gain recognition as vital contributors to the evolutionary ascendance of humanity. But, more importantly, they presented to the world their dissatisfaction with and refutation of the socio-cultural proscription of woman to the role of helpless, weak, and largely ineffectual subordinate to man. Furthermore, these women sought to create a forum/environment from which they could foster unity among women, positively affect the social, economic, and political status of women (nationally and internationally), and claim the right of self-interpretation and definition.

Black Victorian Feminists and the World's Congress of Representative Women

That the discussion of progressive womanhood in this great assemblage of the representative women of the world is considered incomplete without some account of the colored woman's status is a most noteworthy evidence that we have not failed to impress ourselves on the higher side of American life.

—Fannie Barrier Williams, *The Intellectual Progress of the Colored Women of the United States Since the Emancipation Proclamation*

The World's Congress of Representative Women provided a rare opportunity for the 'Black Victorian Feminist delegation' for two reasons. First, they were presented the opportunity to showcase the fruits of Black Victorian Feminist theory and methodology before a national and international audience. Second, while they consistently endeavored to elevate Black womanhood, by necessity if not always desire, the endeavor to uplift the entire Black community could not be divorced from the work to elevate Black womanhood. In this woman's forum they were afforded the opportunity to focus and speak solely on the experience of Black women. And while their individual speeches addressed several topics pertinent to the Black community, their primary focus and theme revolved around the root of Black Victorian Feminist theory and action—the re-claimation and re-formation of Black womanhood. Furthermore, they came before the assemblage not as illiterate and powerless slaves or former slaves, asking for help and/or approval, but as educated, articulate, intelligent women—self-empowered with personal success and achievement as well as the confidence and respect earned through invaluable work as community builders and leaders. They stood on even ground with their fellow white-women-delegates. They could rightfully claim, in some cases, experience superior in education, publication, travel, political, social and economic (employment) activities, to that of their fellow white-women-delegates. In fact, these six Black women delegates held out their lives and experiences—as well as the experiences and achievements of all African American women—as the epitome of the potential of an enlightened progressive womanhood. Fanny Jackson Coppin remarked: "If we have been able to achieve anything by heroic living and thinking, all the more you can achieve it. It is an unanswerable argument for every woman's claim."[347]

Frances Ellen Watkins Harper was the lone African American member of the panel assembled to address the Congress on the Civil and Political Status of

Women. While her address was pertinent to the congress's theme, her address, entitled *Woman's Political Future*, emanated from the perspective of a nineteenth century Black woman who was sure of who and what she was:"…the world has need of all the spiritual aid that woman can give for the social advancement and moral development of the human race."[348] With this opening statement, Harper unequivocally declared to the assemblage, and the world, that there was no doubt about it—African American women were true women and worthy of the title 'Lady.' She did not need to debate or elaborate the particulars. While nineteenth century American women were not fully emancipated, Harper contended that women actually wielded great influence in American society. And that influence was grounded in an enlightened womanhood: "By opening the doors of labor woman has become a rival claimant for at least some of the wealth monopolized by her stronger brother. In the home she is the priestess, in society the queen, in literature she is a power, in legislative halls law-makers have humanized and liberalized their laws. The press has felt the impress of her hand. In the pews of the church she constitutes the majority; the pulpit has welcomed her and in the school she has the blessed privilege of teaching children and youth."[349]

Harper contended that women gaining the right to vote would only further improve home-life and society for America would not only gain more voters, they would be *better* voters. Harper envisioned that the woman's vote was essential in the endeavor to end 'lynch law' and the criminals who committed this atrocity with impunity. Some of the same men who enjoyed the right to vote and participate in all aspects of the political process, while their victims were locked out, were also "…red handed men…who walk[ed] unwhipped of justice…brutal cowardly men, who torture, burn, and lynch their fellow men…"[350] The fact that lynch mobs and their supporters were able to wield societal and political influence (to the detriment of other citizens) while women and African American men were denied basic civil and political rights led Harper to conclude that the social and cultural advancement and moral development of the country was dependant on the up building of national character and the development of a national conscience. Although these same lawless men boasted about the aristocracy of blood, talent, and wealth the aristocracy of conscience and character far outranked them all and "…it is the women of a country who help mold its character, and to influence if not determine its destiny."[351]

Finally, Harper thought that it was unconscionable that socially and politically active white women, in particular—who were demanding a more 'responsible' role/presence in the American political process; who avowed that women's participation in the American political process was essential to the *forward march of civ-*

ilization—were virtually silent about the horrendously brutal and cowardly crime of lynching that was freely committed against a group of American citizens. To these women Harper directed the remark "It is yours to create a healthy public sentiment; to demand justice, simple justice, as the right of every race; to brand with everlasting infamy the lawless and brutal cowardice that lynches, burns, and tortures your own countrymen."[352] Thus, while she embraced the ideals of the Congress, Frances Harper was intent on 'reminding' the assemblage that not only were Black women true women, but the women's movement could not put their collective head in the sand on some issues if they expected to achieve their goals and be full-fledged members of the American political system.

Fannie Barrier Williams was the first of the Black Victorian Feminist delegation to speak to the first of two the topics to be addressed by the Black ladies: *The Intellectual Progress of the Colored Women of the United States Since the Emancipation Proclamation* and *The Organized Efforts of the Colored Women of the South to Improve Their Condition.* Williams began her speech with the observation that not only was Black women's experience under the Slaveocratic regime simultaneously sorrowful and wonderfully heroic but "...it must ever be counted as one of the most wonderful things in human history how promptly and eagerly these suddenly liberated women tried to lay hold upon all there is in human excellence...to taste the blessedness of intelligent womanhood."[353] Nevertheless, the legacy of the supposed taint of immorality on Black women, conferred by the Slaveocratic regime and the larger society, hampered the efforts of Black women to re-claim and re-form American ideas about their womanhood:"...because the morality of our home life has been commented upon so disparagingly and meanly that we have been placed in the unfortunate position of being defenders of our name."[354]

In her efforts to re-claim and re-form Black womanhood before the assemblage, Williams presents Black women's experience not as a monolith but as a multi-layered experience that recognized not only the difference in Black women's experience during the Slaveocracy *but the difference Black women recognized and assigned to their own experience.* Williams delineates three ranges of Black women's experience during the Slaveocracy: free Black women living in the North and the South, enslaved women "...whose force of character enabled them to escape the taints of immorality"[355], and enslaved women who were unable to avoid the worst that the Slaveocracy offered. Williams contended that any discussion of the moral progress, *as defined by the larger society*, of Black women since emancipation only pertained to the latter group of African American women. This latter group, according to Williams, had been trapped in the tentacles of an institution whose lifeblood was the attempted systematic dehumanization, demoralization, and *defeminization* of African American women at the hands of the very entity that purported to define true womanhood—the white community. Williams avowed that, since the Slaveocracy's demise, all three groups had "…so elevated the moral tone of their social life that new and purer standards of personal worth have been created, and new ideals of womanhood, instinct with grace and delicacy, are everywhere recognized and emulated."[356] Williams challenged the assemblage, and the world, to judge African American women not by the standards of the Slaveocracy, but by the higher standards of twenty-five years of freedom, education, culture and moral conduct.

Williams identified education as an essential tool in the endeavor of the attainment of a further enlightened womanhood and the elevation of the entire Black community: "For thirty years education has been the magic word among the colored people in this country. That their greatest need was education in its broadest sense was understood by these people more strongly than it could be taught to them."[357] Moreover, Williams linked Black women's attainment of an education to economic opportunity. She noted that while African American women were eager to contribute to the moral and intellectual forces of American society, they were the recipients of unreasonable discrimination. "They are the only women in the country for whom real ability, virtue, and special talents count for nothing…colored women carefully prepare themselves for all kinds of occupations only to meet with stern refusal, rebuff, and disappointment."[358] Williams warned that the discrimination and denial of opportunity that Black women faced made a mockery of America's highest ideals and threatened the advancement of civilization. Discrimination and the denial of opportunity "…belies every maxim of justice and fair play…[taking] the blessed meaning out of all the teachings of our civilization, and sadly confuses our conceptions of what is just, humane, and moral."[359] On behalf of all African American women, Williams asked that Black women be judged not by race or gender but by individual talent, not only for the betterment of the African American community, but also because: "Colored women are becoming more and more a part of the social forces that must help to determine the questions that so concern women generally."[360] Finally, Williams linked the politically, socially and culturally sanctioned persecution of and injustices against Black women to the overall detriment of the woman's movement. Williams was confident that when the women of the larger society fully recognized the intellectual and moral excellence that was an essential and *constant* element of African American women's experience the result would be "As women of a common experience, with common interests…When you learn that womanhood everywhere among us is blossoming out into greater fullness of everything that is sweet, beautiful, and good in woman…this Congress will at once see the fullness of our fellowship and help us avert the arrows of prejudice that pierce the soul because of the color of our bodies."[361]

Anna Julia Cooper was the next to address the assemblage. While Cooper also acknowledged the wide breadth of African American women's experience, during and after the Slaveocracy, unlike Williams, she firmly located the existence of an ethic of true womanhood *within the enslaved women's community*. Cooper cast enslaved women as heroines of true womanhood, whose experience under the Slaveocracy was "…full of heroic struggle, a struggle against fearful and over-whelming odds, that often ended in horrible death, to maintain and protect that which was dearer than life."[362] And what, according to Cooper, did these women hold dearer than life? Those ideals held most sacred to all women: purity and motherhood. Cooper likened enslaved women to entrapped tigresses who fierce-fully, patiently, painfully, and often *silently* fought "…to gain a free simple title to the bodies of their daughters…[and] to keep hallowed their own persons…"[363] Cooper unabashedly declared that white idealized notions of female passivity and helplessness were absurd, especially in face of the fact that enslaved women, *in their capacity as women and mothers*, were engaged in the battle to retain and maintain their most fundamental claims to womanhood: their sexual selves and the right to protect their children. Furthermore, those who continued to deny that African American women were worthy of the title 'Lady' had been complicit in the effort to obliterate Black womanhood and although"…in the eyes of the highest tribunal in America she [the enslaved woman] was deemed no more than chattel, an irresponsible thing, a dull block, to be drawn hither or thither at the volition of an owner, Afro-American women maintained ideals of womanhood unshamed by any ever conceived."[364]

Since Emancipation, according to Cooper, Black women faced the monumen-tal task of self-powered elevation from the starting point of no education, wealth, political status or influence. Undaunted, Black women began to build a Black community, brick-by-brick, and in the process diffused throughout their fledg-ling community: "…a contagious longing for higher living and purer thinking, inspiring woman herself with a new sense of her dignity…"[365] In her conclusion, Cooper delivered a pointed message to the assemblage on behalf of her constitu-ency—African American women. Cooper avowed that the recognition of Black women as true women was essential to the ultimate success of the woman's move-ment as a whole because all women were, on some level, 'true women.' Thus, "…woman's cause is one and universal…not till the universal title of humanity to life, liberty, and the pursuit of happiness is conceded to be inalienable to all, not till then is woman's lesson taught and woman's cause won..."[366]

Fannie Jackson Coppin was the final woman to speak to the topic of the intellectual progress of Black women. Coppin's short speech primarily focused on the educational aspirations of African American women since Emancipation. Coppin informed the assemblage that Black women's desire for an education came from "...the desire to know, not just a little, but a great deal...not merely to gain an honest livelihood but from a God-given love of all that is beautiful and best and because we thought we could do it."[367] As with her two predecessors, Coppin indelibly linked Black women's strivings to be and do more with all women's aspirations to be and do more than those more powerful and influential than they deemed 'appropriate' and 'realistic': "You know yourselves you have been met with a great many arguments of that kind. Why educate the woman—what will she do with it? An impertinent question, and an unwise one. Rather ask, What will she be with it?"[368]

Sarah Jane Early and Hallie Quinn Brown addressed the second topic before the Congress on the Solidarity of Human Interests: *The Organized Efforts of the Colored Women of the South to Improve Their Condition.* Sarah Jane Early was the first to speak before the assemblage: "...men begin to think, and thought brings revolution, and revolution changes the condition of men and leads them into a happier and brighter existence. So have the great revolutions of the age affected the condition of the colored people of the Southern states..."[369] Early informed the assemblage that although the end of slavery had left African Americans homeless, destitute and 'robbed of every inheritance save their trust in God,' they were, for the first time, free to follow the grand impulse innate in all humanity; to raise themselves "to that degree of intellectual and moral excellence which a wise and beneficient Creator designed that he should enjoy."[370]

Early then began to chronicle the evolution of the African American community, locating the bedrock of this community in the church, Black organizations and institutions. Early observed that the advancement of Black womanhood had evolved in tandem with the newly freed Black community. While she included the community building and leadership activities of Black women within an overarching theme of the coalescence of the Black community, Early gave particular attention to what she indicated as one of most important endeavors of Black women's activism: "screening [African American women] from the stinging arrows of the tongue of slander and the carping criticisms of a relentless foe."[371] In addition, Black women's organizations provided an environment where Black women could learn and teach the art of self-government, business and other vital methods of Black women's self-empowerment that, in turn, provided Black women the ways and means of rescuing themselves from a condition of helplessness and destitution to a state of self-dependence and greater opportunity for personal and communal prosperity. Early avowed that not only was Black womanhood true but had quickly become a force to be reckoned with: "now they stand in a grand sisterhood, nearly one million strong, bound together by the strongest ties of which the human mind can conceive..."[372] Thus, in comparing the present condition of the Black people of the South to their condition under slavery, just twenty-eight years in the past, according to Early it was clearly evident the essential contribution that Black women and their organizational efforts had made to the 'marvelous' elevation of the 'race' in such a short period of time. And that marvelous elevation was illustrated by the great strides the African Americans had made in education—not only educational achievement but the construction and maintenance of Black schools and colleges, land and business ownership, as well as a myriad of strong successful Black inspired, executed and maintained institutions.

Early ended her address with the self-effacing observation that while her audience, with their hundreds of years of wealth, education, power and opportunity, may view Black women's successful efforts at organization and self-improvement as feeble and insignificant, the coalescence and advancement of the Black community had been wrought by a group of people only twenty-eight years removed from nearly three centuries of slavery: "If we in the midst of poverty and proscription can aspire to a noble destiny...what may we not accomplish in the day of prosperity?"[373] And on the heels of this self-effacement came an ominous prediction. Over the past twenty-eight years, hundreds of thousands of Black women had been involved in the successful struggle to improve their minds and their lot. Early predicted that these women, with all of the knowledge and power of a modern civilization, "which have a tendency to enlighten the mind and cultivate the heart," would populate the next generation of enlightened Black womanhood, "perfect that system of organization among their race of which they themselves are the first fruits," break through into the larger society and bring their families and their community with them.[374]

Hallie Quinn Brown was the last Black woman to speak before the World's Congress of Representative Women. The Board of Lady Managers may have intended the participation of the African American women's delegation at the Congress to be grist for the discourse of exoticism that pervaded the Exposition, in a further attempt to legitimate the racist assumptions of the larger society, but they got much more than they bargained for! These women were not only *not* representative denizens of some exotic other world, they were engaged in a public and political, collective and tangible act of identity re-claimation and re-formation; an act of *willed creation*. While all of the speeches of these Black Victorian Feminists were such acts, Brown's address cut out the heart and guts of the larger society's construction of Black womanhood and offered it for national and international consumption.

Brown contended that tenets of true womanhood were as innate in the African American woman as in women from the larger society so much so that the larger society, under the Slaveocratic regime, had mightily attempted to kill this natural impulse through two hundred and fifty years of systematic demoralization, degradation and defeminization. Moreover the assignment of an innate lack of morality and innate sexual promiscuity to enslaved women at the hands of the larger society was based not in truth or fact, but in two motivations—avarice and financial gain: "Side by side with the men of her race she toiled in the dank rice-swamps, in the cotton-fields, and the lone cane-breaks. She tilled the soil of her so-called master, enlarged his estates, heaped his coffers with shining gold, and filled his home with the splendors of the world."[375] For personal and national financial gain and power the larger society chose to count the Black woman as "little higher than the brute creation that surrounded her, and was said to possess neither a brain nor a soul."[376] Yet enslaved women had brains, souls, and hearts; and they used them to maintain a sense of self and create and maintain a Black woman's community.

The demise of the Slaveocracy, according to Brown, not only signaled the end to slavery but also simultaneously heralded the beginning of the next phase in the evolution of Black feminism and intellectual enterprise. "And when…the gyves and chains on wrists and ankles were broken she stepped forth, her body scarred and striped by the lash, her intellect dwarfed and sunken into piteous ignorance, without money, clothes, or a home—but a free woman."[377] According to Brown, the first impulse of these newly free Black women was to re-claim their true womanhood. And although those in power predicted that the African American woman would never be able to transcend beyond her supposedly immutably brutish and unwomanly nature, in only twenty-eight years: "the Afro-American woman advanced beyond the most sanguine expectations…through unremitting exertions she has climbed to elevated planes, accepting all which dignifies and refines, and flourishing under it."[378]

Asserting that Black womanhood ever endeavored to transcend, Brown informed the assemblage that although the holocaust embodied in the Slaveocracy had weakened the intellect and dwarfed the faculties of Black women, a scant twenty-eight years had passed and "what are thirty years in the history of a nation? It is but a day…"[379] Brown avowed that with the proper care and enough time, the educated Black woman, by her very existence, would put to rest all claims of Black women's incapacity and inferiority. It would be self-evident when "…the centuries of her hideous servitude have been succeeded by centuries of education, culture, and refinement by which she may rise to the fullness of the stature of her highest ideal."[380] Finally, Brown envisioned a day when her white counterparts, already mightily strengthened by their centuries of wealth, education and social position, would unite with African American women and together they would bring about the elevation of all women.

The presence and participation of these seven Black Victorian Feminists at the Columbian Exposition of 1893 is not necessarily the most radical moment in nineteenth century Black Feminist discourse. Their participation did not herald a monumental change in Black Feminist theory, it was the progenitor. Their presence and participation at the Exposition was an exemplar of how Black feminist theory and action would be represented and disseminated to the nation and the world. Identity re-claimation and re-formation and confirmation of the existence of a viable Black womanhood are endeavors that are constant throughout African American women's experience, discourse and intellectual production. But until the advent of Black Victorian Feminism and the Black Woman's Era these endeavors primarily operated behind a veil of dissemblance that worked in conjunction with the general invisibility of Black women from the larger society. What renders these seven ladies actions at the Exposition new and innovative was that they *purposely stepped out from behind the protective veil of dissemblance and stepped up and onto a podium before a national and international audience—staked their claim, raised their voices, invisible no longer, silent no longer, silenced no longer.* Moreover, six of these 'Ladies' were instrumental in the codification Black Feminist theory. Hallie Quinn Brown's *Homespun Heroines and Other Women of Distinction*, Anna Julia Cooper's *A Voice from the South*, Fanny Jackson Coppin's *Reminiscences of School Life and Hints on Teaching*, Frances Harper's *Iola Leroy*, Ida B. Wells's *Southern Horrors*, and Fannie Barrier Williams's "The Colored Girl," "The Woman's Part in a Man's Business," and "The Problem of Employment for Negro Women," became the blueprint from which their contemporaries and future generations of Black Feminists would find their own voices and further shape Black Feminist discourse and intellectual enterprise.

I began the research and composition of this dissertation with a clear and firm theoretical premise: African American women's history is a singular phenomenon with definite characteristics. This premise is grounded in the fact that although this experience is heterogeneous, African American women share a common experience of racism, sexism and classism—a triad of oppression. In turn, this common experience suggests four core themes: the legacy of struggle, the search for voice, the interdependence of thought and action, and the importance of empowerment in everyday life. Furthermore, through examination of this triad of oppression and these four core common historical themes, within the context of an ever evolving and distinct Black female consciousness—that, in turn, produced a feminist-intellectual discourse—the roots of Black Victorian Feminism would be revealed.

Excavating Nineteenth Century Black Womanhood

I am a black woman.
Tall as a cypress,
Strong beyond all definition,
Still defying place and time and circumstance.
Assailed.
Impervious.
Indestructible.
Look upon me and be renewed.

—Mari Evans, *I Am a Black Woman*

My goal was multifaceted: to locate the genesis of a 'grassroots' mode of Black feminism within the enslaved women's community during the Slaveocracy; to trace its evolution through the antebellum free Black community; and reveal the contours of its further evolution from Reconstruction to the turn-of-the-century. And finally to identify, at a specific moment in American history, when this 'grassroots' articulation of Black feminism transcended into a Black Victorian Feminist discourse and intellectual enterprise. The culmination of a particular era in Black women's history was illustrated by Black Victorian Feminists' palpable presence at the Columbian Exposition of 1893—a moment that simultaneously heralded the next phase in Black women's history.

My methodological approach to the analysis of Black women's participation at the Exposition, too, was clear and firm. In the endeavor to shift the paradigm of 'traditional' American historical scholarship and tell a new story I would place the Black woman in the role of protagonist and chiefly use the primary and secondary sources produced by and focused on African American women—thereby creating a fresh framework where a Black feminist viewpoint was embedded in categories of analysis, in notions of historical significance, in beliefs about who the important actors are, and in the causal logic of the story. Through this theoretical and methodological approach I was able to excavate the truly fascinating and extraordinary world of the nineteenth century Black woman. Moreover, I was able to locate, excavate, and examine a distinct and profound sub-group in American history—Black Victorian Feminists.

These cultural producers and transmitters, community builders, leaders, and activists embarked on an individual and communal quest for the acquisition of power—through a doctrine based in the concept of the elevation of Black womanhood; an ideology of racial solidarity; a historical foundation of a Black feminist ethos; and a unique Victorian sensibility. Through unconventional means and conventional means used unconventionally, these articulate, educated, self-made women—only twenty-eight years removed from slavery—built a viable Black community, its institutions and organizations. Yet for all of their trials and tribulations, triumphs and disappointments, production and development of a feminist discourse and intellectual enterprise, they remained trapped within the antebellum ideology of gender and race. Gail Bederman posits that, because of the contradictions inherent in any ideology, men and women are able to influence the ongoing ideological process: "[women] can combine and recombine them, exploit the contradictions between them, and work to modify them. They can also alter their position in relations to these ideologies."[381] In the end, however, they cannot escape them.

The dominating gender ideology of the Slaveocracy (also known as the cult of true womanhood) represented the greatest post-slavery obstacle to Black women's quest for personal autonomy and unfettered economic and social opportunity. The power of the ideology of true womanhood did not emanate from its veracity. Clearly very few white women, during or after the Slaveocracy—in the South or North—could not apply the tenets of true womanhood to their daily lives. The generative power of this ideology is not to be found in its accuracy or authenticity (or the lack thereof), but in the fact that this ideology represented a cultural stranglehold as the ultimate arbiter of what constituted a Lady, a woman, and true womanhood. Hazel V. Carby observed that one of the most confounding and frustrating aspects of the cult of true womanhood, for nineteenth century Black women and their historians, is that while Black women existed outside the boundaries of true womanhood, "…black female sexuality was nevertheless used to define what those boundaries were."[382] Thus, while the ideology of true womanhood may have been subverted by white women, overtime, to better suit their purposes, "the links between black women and illicit sexuality consolidated during the antebellum years had powerful ideological consequences for the next one hundred and fifty years."[383] In addition to the humiliation wrought by the power and prevalence of a denigrated Black womanhood, the exclusion of Black women from the ideology of true womanhood was a major tool used by the larger society to politically and economically subjugate and oppress African Americans. Thus, in order to fully and freely partake in the American Dream as well as rescue Black womanhood from the taint of sexual immorality, the first and ultimately overriding endeavor of Black Victorian Feminist theory and action was to confront the dominant cultural gender ideology and reconstruct it in order to produce an alternate discourse of late nineteenth century Black womanhood.

In the end, I do not believe that Brown, Cooper, Coppin, Early, Harper, Wells and Williams were trying to escape the ideology of gender. I believe that their intent was to re-configure this ideology in order to secure a recognized space for Black women within it, an intellectual and cultural space for Black women. From within this space the true breadth and depth of Black women's voices and experiences could be discovered, exchanged and debated along with the multitude of men and women's voices and experiences that formed the American population. Like the larger society, these ladies believed in and celebrated the unique role that women played in their society. Yet they were also well aware of the interrelation of racial and sexual oppression and were exemplars of the ways in which Black women intellectuals and community activists were "analyzing particular forms of oppression in an attempt to define the political parameters of gender, race and patriarchal authority."[384] This motley group of Black women who made their presence known and felt at the Columbian Exposition of 1893 wholeheartedly embraced the commitment to fostering and advancing women's intellectual activity, recognition of women's contribution to the advancement of civilization, the realization of the procurement of empowering changes for women around the world, and the creation of a forum from which the unity of all women could be realized. Yet they had an even more far-reaching agenda—the unencumbered recognition and acceptance of African American women as true women, in their own right, and the application of these same aspirations and goals to the entire African American community. Before a national and international audience, for the first time, these ladies offered to the world an emergent Black Victorian Feminist discourse and intellectual enterprise that was produced from a distinct consciousness, culture and experience. Unique, complex and contradictorary, these ladies boldly and courageously stepped up to the lectern and lifted their interwoven voices into the multi-layered tapestry representative of nineteenth century Black womanhood.

ENDNOTES

<u>CHAPTER ONE</u>

[1] Throughout the rest of this dissertation I will refer to the Columbian Exposition of 1893, held in Chicago, as the Exposition.

[2] I use the terms African American and Black interchangeably. Both refer to people of African descent who reside in the United States.

[3] Hazel V. Carby, *Reconstructing Womanhood: The Emergence of the Afro-American Woman Novelist* (New York: Oxford University Press, 1987), 5.

[4] Patricia Hill Collins, "Feminism in the 20th Century," in *Black Women in America*, ed. Darlene Clark Hine, Elsa Barkley Brown and Rosalyn Terborg Penn (Indiana University Press, 1993), 416.

[5] Ibid., 418.

[6] Ibid., 418.

[7] Patricia Hill Collins, "Learning from the Outsider Within: The Sociological Significance of Black Feminist Thought," in *Social Problems* (December 1986) Vol. 33, No. 6, page S14.

[8] Brenda E. Stevenson, "Gender Convention, Ideals, and Identity Among Antebellum Virginia Slave Women," in *More Than Chattel: Black Women and Slavery in the Americas*, ed. David Barry Gaspar and Darlene Clark Hine (University of Indiana Press, 1996).

[9] Patricia Hill Collins, "Feminism in the Twentieth Century," 419.

[10] Ibid., 419.

[11] Darlene Clark Hine, "Rape and the Inner Lives of Black Women in the Middle West: Preliminary Thoughts on the Culture of Dissemblance," In *Unequal*

Sisters, ed. Vicki L. Ruiz and Ellen Carol Dubois, 342-347. (New York: Routledge, 1994), 343.

[12] Deborah Grey White, *Ar'n't I A Woman?: Female Slaves in the Plantation South* (New York: W.W. Norton and Co., 1999), 44.

[13] Christopher Reed, *All the World is Here!: The Black Presence at White City* (Indiana University Press, 2000), ix.

[14] Ibid. xi.

[15] For further discussion on shifting traditional paradigms of American historical inquiry and African American women's place within it see: Patricia Hill Collins "Learning from the Outsider Within: The Sociological Significance of Black Feminist Thought" in *Social Problems* (December 1986) Vol. 33, No. 6, S14-S32; and Tessie Liu, "Teaching the Differences Among Women from a Historical Perspective: Rethinking Race and Gender as Social Categories," in *Unequal Sisters*, ed. Vicki L. Ruiz and Ellen Carol DuBois (New York: Routledge, 1994) 343.

[16] Tessie Liu, "Teaching the Differences Among Women from a Historical Perspective: Rethinking Race and Gender as Social Categories," in *Unequal Sisters*, ed. Vicki L. Ruiz and Ellen Carol DuBois (New York: Routledge, 1994) 573.

[17] Tessie Liu, "Teaching the Differences Among Women from a Historical Perspective," 573.

[18] Deborah Grey White, *Ar'n't I A Woman?: Female Slaves in the Plantation South*, revised edition (New York: W.W. Norton & Co., 1999) 4.

[19] The term *Slaveocracy* refers to that despicable era, in American history, during which Africans and African Americans were confined legally, culturally, religiously, and socially to perpetual enslavement (where they were economically and sexually exploited through the use of indiscriminate and ritualized beatings, torture, coerced sex, and outright rape). This nomenclature is literally the combination of the terms *slave* (a human being who is owned by another human being) and—*cracy* (those who rule through a specific form of government). The era of Slaveocracy, in America, lasted for nearly 300 years: 1641–1865.

CHAPTER TWO

[20] Brenda E. Stevenson, "Slavery," in *Black Women in America*, ed. Darlene Clark Hine, Elsa Barkley Brown and Rosalyn Terborg Penn (Indiana University Press, 1993) 1046.

[21] James Oakes, *Slavery and Freedom*, (New York: W.W. Norton & Co., 1990) 5.

[22] Ibid. 5.

[23] Deborah Gray White, *Ar'n't I A Woman: Female Slaves in the Plantation South*, (New York: W.W. Norton & Company, 1999) 29.

[24] Ibid 35. Also see: Jordon D. Winthrop, *White Over Black: American Attitudes Toward the Negro, 1550–1812* (Chapel Hill: University of North Carolina Press, 1968).

[25] Also see: Egypt S. Ophelia et. al. *Unwritten History of Slavery* (1972); B.A. Boten, *Lay My Burden Down: A Folk History of Slavery* (1945); and, Anne Frances Kemble, *Journal of a Residence on a Georgian Plantation* (1961).

[26] New Orleans seems to have been the center of the trade, but "fancy girls" could be found in other cities, especially Charleston, St. Louis, and Lexington. For further discussion of the Fancy Trade see: Frederic Bancroft, *Slave Trading in the Old South* (New York: Frederic Ungar, 1931).

[27] Deborah Grey White, *Ar'n't I A Woman?*, 38.

[28] Deborah Grey White, *Ar'n't I A Woman?*, 44. Also see: Dr. William Gilmore Simms, "The Morals of Slavery," in *Pro-Slavery Arguments*.

[29] Deborah Grey White, *Ar'n't' I A Woman?*, 60.

For further discussion on Jezebel and Mammy, see: William Drayton, *The South Vindicated from the Treason and Fanaticism of the Northern Abolitionists* (Philadelphia: H. Manley, 1836); Mrs. Nicholas Ware Eppes, *The Negro of the Old South* (Chicago: Joseph G. Branch, 1925); Susan Smedes, *Memorials of a Southern Planter* (New York: Knopf, 1968); Caroline Gilman, *Recollections of a Southern Mistress* (New York: Harper and Brothers, 1938); and Ruth H. Block, "American Feminine Ideals in Transition: The Rise of the Moral Mother, 1785–1815 in *Feminist Studies* (June 1978) 4:101-126.

[30] White acknowledges that any study that concentrates solely on women runs the risk of overstating their roles and their importance. Therefore, her study explores *one critical aspect of slave community life.* "Female Slaves: Sex Roles and Status in the Antebellum South" is a synthesis of the probable sex role of the average slave woman on a plantation with at least 20 slaves. In the process of constructing her synthesis, White takes into account such variables as plantation size, crop, region in the South, and the personal "idiosyncrasies" of slave owners.

In drawing conclusions about the sex role and status of enslaved women, White details their activities and analyzes them in terms of what anthropologists know about women who do similar things in analogous settings. She does so for two reasons: first, detailed information about the lives of enslaved women cannot be discerned because enslaved women left few primary sources. Thus the dearth of primary sources makes it impossible to draw conclusions about enslaved women's feelings. Second, even given analysis of their individual personalities (i.e. through investigation of slave narratives) it is difficult to draw widespread general conclusions about enslaved women's roles. In this work, White examines only the activities of enslaved women in an effort to discern their status in Black society under the Slaveocracy.

Source: Deborah Gray White "Female Slaves: Sex Roles in the Antebellum South." In *Unequal Sisters*, ed. Vicki L. Ruiz and Ellen Carol Dubois, 20-32. New York: Routledge, 1994.

[31] "In the Cotton Belt they plowed fields; dropped seed; and hoed, picked, ginned, sorted, moted cotton. On farms in Virginia, North Carolina, Kentucky, and Tennessee, they hoed tobacco; laid worm fences; and threshed, raked, and bound wheat. For those on the Sea Islands and in coastal areas, rice culture included raking and burning of stubble from the previous year's crop; ditching; sowing seed; plowing, listing, and hoeing fields; and harvesting, stacking, and threshing the rice. In the bayou region of Louisiana, women planted sugar cane cuttings, plowed, and helped to harvest and gin the cane. During the winter, they repaired roads, pitched hay, burned brush, and set up post and rail fences; enslaved women watered horses, fed the chickens, and slopped the hogs. They also ginned cotton, ground hominy, shelled corn and peas, and milled flour." As for work in the 'Big House,' the equally paradoxical nature of the enslaved Black woman's experience of *domesticity* becomes apparent when considering the remembrances by a former slave, Mingo White, of his mother's typical work day: "…[she] served as personal maid to the master's daughter, cooked for all the

hands on the plantation, carded cotton, spun a daily quota of thread, wove and dyed the cloth. Every Wednesday she carried the white family's laundry three-quarters of a mile to a creek where she beat each garment with a wooden paddle. Ironing consumed the rest of her day. Like the lowliest field hand, she felt the lash if any tasks went undone."

Source: Jacqueline Jones, *Labor of Love, Labor of Sorrow*

[32] Jacqueline Jones, *Labor of Love, Labor of Sorrow: Black Women, Work and the Family, From Slavery to the Present* (New York: Vintage Books, 1985) 15.

[33] Deborah Gray White specifically uses the anthropological work of: Leith Mullings, "Women and Economic Change in Africa," in *Halfkin* (1976); Karen Sacks, "Engels Revisited: Women, The Organization of Private Property," in *Rosaldo Lamphere* (1974); Claire Robertson, "Ga Women and Socioeconomic Change in Africa," in *Halfkin* (1976); Nancy Tanner, "Matrifocality in Indonesia and Africa Among Black Americans," in *Rosaldo and Lamphere* (1974); John A. Noon, *Law and Government in the Grand River Iroquois* (New York: Viking, 1949); and, Michele Rosaldo, "Women, Culture, and Society: A Theoretical Overview" in *Rosaldo and Lamphere* (1974).

[34] Cases in point, in Nashville, Tennessee, an enslaved woman named Sally (1790–1849) used her savings to start a successful soap manufacture, laundry and cleaning business. In 1819, Amelia Galle of Petersburg, Virginia inherited the bathhouse that she had managed for her enslaver. Other manumitted enslaved women, who possessed expertise as seamstresses, dressmakers, and milliners ran successful business on property acquired from their former enslavers. And, in some cases, 'mistresses' deeded property to their former 'slaves' providing the opportunity for these entrepreneurial Black women to establish inns, restaurants, and cleaning businesses.

Source: Juliet E.K. Walker, "Entrepreneurs in Antebellum America"

[35] Deborah Grey White, "Female Slaves: Sex Roles in the Antebellum South," in *Unequal Sisters*, ed. Vicki L. Ruiz and Ellen Carol DuBois (New York: Routledge, 1994) 21.

[36] Deborah Grey White, "Female Slaves: Sex Roles in the Antebellum South," 25.

[37] Deborah Grey White, "Female Slaves: Sex Roles in the Antebellum South," 26.

[38] Brenda E. Stevenson, "Gender Convention, Ideals, and Identity Among Antebellum Virginia Slave Women," in *More Than Chattel: Black Women and Slavery in the Americas*, ed. David Barry Gaspar and Darlene Clark Hine (University of Indiana Press, 1996) 169.

Stevenson's primary source: Charles L. Perdue, Thomas E. Barden, and Robert K. Phillips eds., *Weevils in the Wheat: Interviews with Virginia Ex-Slaves* (University Press of Virginia, 1996—a collection of Federal Writers Project interviews of Virginia ex-slaves.

[39] Brenda E. Stevenson, "Gender Convention, Ideals, and Identity Among Antebellum Virginia Slave Women," 171.

[40] Deborah Gray White, *Ar'n't I A Woman?*, 7.

[41] Leonard P. Curry, *The Free Black in Urban America, 1800–1850* (University of Chicago Press, 1981), 3.

[42] Ibid, 3.

[43] Ibid, xix.

[44] Ibid. xix.

[45] Journeyman—One who has served an apprenticeship in a trade and works in another's employ.

Apprentice—One learning a trade under a skilled master.

Artisan—A skilled manual worker.

Master—One who possesses the most skill in his/her chosen trade.

Source: American Heritage Dictionary (New York: Dell Publishing, 1992)

[46] Ibid 19.

[47] Ibid. 35.

[48] Ibid. 35.

[49] Ibid. 35.

[50] Brenda E. Stevenson, "The Abolition Movement," in *Black Women in America* ed. Darlene Clark Hine, Elsa Barkley Brown, and Rosalyn Terborg-Penn (Indiana University Press, 1993), 4.

[51] Brenda E. Stevenson, "The Abolition Movement," 4.

[52] Leonard P. Curry, *The Free Black in Urban America*, 83.

[53] Leonard P. Curry, *The Free Black in Urban America*, 94.

[54] Leonard P. Curry, *The Free Black in Urban America*, 24.

[55] Fannie Barrier Williams, "Religious Duty to the Negro," in *World's Parliament of Religions, Chicago, 1893*: *The World's Congress of Religions* (Chicago, 1894) 895.

[56] Leonard P. Curry, *The Free Black in Urban America*, 175.

[57] Leonard P. Curry, *The Free Black in Urban America*, 191.

[58] Leonard P. Curry, *The Free Black in Urban America*, 195.

[59] Evelyn Brooks Higginbotham, "African American Women's History and the Metalanguage of Race," in *We Specialize in the Wholly Impossible* ed. Darlene Clark Hine, Wilma King and Linda Reed (New York: Carlson Publishing, 1995), 5.

[60] Evelyn Brooks Higginbotham, "African American Women's History and the Metalanguage of Race," 7.

[61] Leonard P. Curry, *The Free Black in Urban America*, 200.

[62] Leonard P. Curry, *The Free Black in Urban America*, 214.

[63] Leonard P. Curry, *The Free Black in Urban America*, 149.

[64] Leonard P. Curry, *The Free Black in Urban America*, 149.

[65] Leonard P. Curry, *The Free Black in Urban America*, 173.

[66] Frederick Douglass, "Introduction," in *The Reason Why the Colored American Is Not in the World's Columbian Exposition* in *Women and Social Movements, 1775–2000* © by Thomas Dublin and Kathryn Kish Sklar.

[67] Leonard P. Curry, *The Free Black in Urban America*, 225.

[68] Leonard P. Curry, *The Free Black in Urban America*, 229.

[69] Leonard P. Curry, *The Free Black in Urban America*, 230.

[70] Reference to the uprising in 1791 by Black slaves on the Caribbean island of Saint Dominique. It began as a rebellion against enslavement that eventually "...destroyed the dominant white population, the plantation system, and the institution of slavery in the most prosperous colony of the Western hemisphere." What began as a slave revolt evolved into a thirteen year long political revolution that ultimately resulted in the colony gaining independence from France and the establishment of the first independent Black republic in the world—the republic of Haiti.

Source: "Haitian Revolution," Microsoft ® Encarta ® Africana © & (p) 1999 Microsoft Corporation.

[71] By 1860, more than 260,000 free African Americans lived in the south, 53% of which were women. Adele Alexander and Virginia Gould posit that an enslaved Black woman was more likely to manumitted (through will, deed, self purchase, or legislative act) than an enslaved Black man, primarily because the white population viewed women as less threatening to the social order.

Source: Adele Logan Alexander and Virginia Gould, "Free Black Women in the Antebellum South," in *Black Women in America*, eds., Darlene Clark Hine, Elsa Barkley Brown, and Rosalyn Terborg Penn (Indiana University Press, 1993) 458.

[72] Adele Logan Alexander and Virginia Gould, "Free Black Women in the Antebellum South," 456.

[73] The Cane River region of Louisiana, and the Chasing Bluff and Mon Luis Islands communities are examples of rural communities where African Americans (and other peoples of color) lived and thrived. During the Slaveocracy, a thriving Creole community was established. They were the racially mixed descendents of

African, French, and Spanish settlers of colonial Louisiana and Florida who identified themselves as 'free Creoles of color.' For the most part, Creoles were socially
and legally recognized as free citizens. Louisiana Creoles became U.S. residents
following the Louisiana Purchase (1803). By 1860, approximately 20,000 Creoles lived in the lower South.

Source: Adele Logan Alexander and Virginia Gould, "Free Black Women in the
Antebellum South," 458.

[74] Brenda E. Stevenson, "The Abolition Movement," 4.

[75] In "To Earn Her Daily Bread: Housework and Antebellum Working-Class
Subsistence" (1994), Jeanne Boydston argues that antebellum working class and
poor families relied on subsistence means in order to supplement wages. Moreover, a key economic resource was housework itself. In order to gauge the
exchange value of housework, Boydston equivocates housework with "domestic
service" fees paid in the antebellum period. Boydston estimates that women's
household labor (Black and white) produced as much as half of a working class or
poor family's subsistence.

[76] Jeanne Boydston, "To Earn Her Daily Bread: Housework and Antebellum
Working-Class Subsistence," in *Unequal Sisters*, ed. Vicki L. Ruiz and Ellen
Carol DuBois (New York: Routledge, 1994), 49.

[77] Jeanne Boydston, "To Earn Her Daily Bread: Housework and Antebellum
Working-Class Subsistence," 49.

[78] Jeanne Boydston, "To Earn Her Daily Bread: Housework and Antebellum
Working-Class Subsistence," 50.

[79] Juliet E.K. Walker, "Entrepreneurs in Antebellum America" in *Black Women
in America*, ed. Darlene Clark Hine, Elsa Barkley Brown and Rosalyn Terborg
Penn (Indiana University Press, 1993) 397.

[80] Julie Winch, "You Have Talents—Only Cultivate Them: Philadelphia's Black
Female Literary Societies and the Abolitionist Crusade," in *The Abolitionist Sisterhood: Women's Political Culture in Antebellum America* (New York: Cornell University Press, 1994), 101.

[81] Julie Winch "You Have Talents—Only Cultivate Them," 102.

[82] Willie Coleman, "Architects of a Vision: Black Women and Their Antebellum Quest for Political and Social Equality" in *African American Women and the Vote, 1831–1965* ed. Ann D. Gordon (University of Massachusetts Press, 1997) 26.

[83] Willie Coleman, "Architects of a Vision," 26.

[84] Brenda E. Stevenson "The Abolition Movement," 5.

[85] Willie Coleman, "Architects of a Vision," 29.

[86] Willie Coleman, "Architects of a Vision," 30.

[87] Anne M. Boylan "Benevolence and Antislavery Activity Among African American Women in New York and Boston, 1820–1840" in *The Abolitionist Sisterhood: Women's Political Culture in Antebellum America* (Cornell University Press, 1994) 130.

[88] Julie Winch "You Have Talents—Only Cultivate Them," 105.

[89] Julie Winch "You Have Talents—Only Cultivate Them," 105.

[90] Julie Winch "You Have Talents—Only Cultivate Them," 103.

[91] Julie Winch "You Have Talents—Only Cultivate Them," 108.

[92] Julie Winch "You Have Talents—Only Cultivate Them," 110.

[93] Susan A. Taylor, "Colored Females Free Produce Society" in *Black Women in America* ed. Darlene Clark Hine, Elsa Barkley Brown, and Rosalyn Terborg-Penn (Indiana University Press, 1993) 266.

[94] Susan A. Taylor, "Colored Females Free Produce Society," 267.

[95] Anne M. Boylan "Benevolence and Antislavery Activity Among African American Women in New York and Boston, 1820–1840," 120.

[96] Anne M. Boylan "Benevolence and Antislavery Activity Among African American Women in New York and Boston, 1820–1840," 132.

[97] Anne M. Boylan "Benevolence and Antislavery Activity Among African American Women in New York and Boston, 1820–1840," 123.

[98] Brenda E. Stevenson "The Abolition Movement," 6.

[99] Darlene Clark Hine, "Rape and the Inner Lives of Black Women in the Middle West: Preliminary Thoughts on the Culture of Dissemblance," in *Unequal Sisters*, eds., Vicki L. Ruiz and Ellen Carol DuBois (New York: Routledge, 1994) 343.

[100] Evelyn Brooks Higginbotham, *Righteous Discontent* (New York: Harvard University Press, 1993) 5.

[101] Evelyn Brooks Higginbotham, *Righteous Discontent*, 5.

[102] Evelyn Brooks Higginbotham, *Righteous Discontent*, 49.

[103] Evelyn Brooks Higginbotham, *Righteous Discontent*, 49.

[104] Darlene Clark Hine, "Rape and the Inner Lives of Black Women in the Middle West," 312.

[105] Deborah Grey White, *Ar'n't I A Woman?*, 9.

[106] Darlene Clark Hine, "Rape and the Inner Lives of Black Women in the Middle West," 314.

[107] Darlene Clark Hine, "Rape and the Inner Lives of Black Women in the Middle West," 152.

[108] Evelyn Brooks Higginbotham, "African American Women's History and the Metalanguage of Race," in *We Specialize in the Wholly Impossible* eds., Darlene Clark Hine, Wilma King, and Linda Reed (New York: Carlson Publishing, 1995) 10.

[109] Darlene Clark Hine, "Rape and the Inner Lives of Black Women in the Middle West," 345.

[110] Evelyn Brooks Higginbotham, *Righteous Discontent*, 10.

[111] Sharon Harley, "The Middle Class" in *Black Women in America* eds. Darlene Clark Hine, Elsa Barkley Brown and Rosalyn Terborg Penn (Indiana University Press, 1993) 786.

[112] Sharon Harley, "The Middle Class," 787.

[113] Sharon Harley, "The Middle Class," 788.

[114] Evelyn Brooks Higginbotham, *Righteous Discontent*, 56.

[115] Evelyn Brooks Higginbotham, "African-American Women's History and the Metalanguage of Race," 14.

[116] Evelyn Brooks Higginbotham, "African-American Women's History and the Metalanguage of Race," 8.

CHAPTER THREE

[117] Ellen NicKensie Lawson, *The Three Sarahs: Documents of Antebellum Black College Women* (New York: Edwin Mellen Press, 1984) 150.

[118] Ellen NicKensie Lawson, *The Three Sarahs*, 151.

[119] Ellen NicKensie Lawson, *The Three Sarahs*, 152.

[120] Ellen NicKensie Lawson, *The Three Sarahs*, 15.

[121] Marlene Deahl Merril "Oberlin College" in *Black Women in America* eds Darlene Clark Hine, Elsa Barkley Brown and Rosalyn Terborg-Penn (Indiana University Press, 1993) 897.

[122] Marlene Deahl Merril "Oberlin College" 898.

[123] Marlene Deahl Merril "Oberlin College" 898.

[124] Robin Wilson "Introduction" in *Women Builders, Tales My Father Told, Pen Pictures of Wilberforce*, Hallie Quinn Brown and Sadie Iola Daniel (New York: G.K. Hall & Co., 1997) xxiv.

[125] Robin Wilson "Introduction" in *Women Builders*, xxv.

[126] The Bureau of Refugees, Freedmen and Abandoned Lands was created by the federal government in March 1865. It soon came to be known as the Freedman's Bureau. The purpose of the Bureau was to provide "…food, clothing, and fuel for the relief of destitute refugees and freed slaves." Over seven years the bureau distributed "…21 million rations to poor whites and free blacks, provided medi-

cal services to another million, and attempted to help ease the transition from slavery to freedom.

Source: Alonford James Robinson, Jr., "Bureau of Refugees, Freedmen, and Abandoned Lands," Microsoft ® Encarta ® Africana. © & (p) 1999 Microsoft Corporation.

[127] Jordan Winston Early was born a slave and was emancipated in 1826 when he was ten years old. Unlike Sarah Jane, Jordan was illiterate. When he was 18 and working on a riverboat, Jordan paid a Presbyterian minister to teach him how to read; and paid a shipmate to teach him how to write. After receiving a preacher's license in St. Louis (1836) Jordan started an African Methodist Episcopalian church there and later started another one in New Orleans.

Source: Ellen NicKensie Lawson, *The Three Sarahs: Documents of Antebellum Black College Women* (New York: Edwin Mellen Press, 1984).

[128] Memphis (1869–1872); Nashville (1872–1875); Edgeefield (1875–1879); Nashville (1880–1884); Columbia (1884–1885); Nashville (1885–1888).

Source: Ellen NicKensie Lawson, *The Three Sarahs: Documents of Antebellum Black College Women* (New York: Edwin Mellen Press, 1984).

[129] Ellen NicKensie Lawson, *The Three* Sarahs, 161.

[130] Sarah Jane Early in *The Three Sarahs: Documents of Antebellum Black College Women*

[131] Sarah Jane Early in *The Three Sarahs: Documents of Antebellum Black College Women* 151.

[132] Sarah Jane Early "Annual Report of the National Woman's Christian Temperance Union, 1889 in *The Three Sarahs*, 171.

[133] Frances Smith Foster, *A Brighter Coming Day* (New York: The Feminist Press, 1990) 7.

[134] Frances Smith Foster, *A Brighter Coming Day*, 7.

[60] Frances Smith Foster, *A Brighter Coming Day*, 7.

[136] Frances Smith Foster, *A Brighter Coming Day*, 7.

[137] Frances Ellen Watkins Harper "The Woman's Christian Temperance Union and the Colored Woman" in *A Brighter Coming Day 281.*

[138] Frances Ellen Watkins Harper "These Lines…the Expiring Flicker of a Lamp" in *A Brighter Coming Day* 324.

[139] Fanny Jackson Coppin, *Reminiscences of School Life and Hints on Teaching* (Philadelphia: African Methodist Episcopal Book Concern, 1913) 10.

[140] Fanny Jackson Coppin, *Reminiscences*, 11.

[141] Fanny Jackson Coppin, *Reminiscences*, 11.

[142] Fanny Jackson Coppin, *Reminiscences*, 17.

[143] Fanny Jackson Coppin, *Reminiscences*, 18.

[144] Fanny Jackson Coppin, *Reminiscences*, 18.

[145] Linda M. Perkins, "Institute for Colored Youth, Philadelphia" in *Black Women in America*, eds. Darlene Clark Hine, Elsa Barkley and Rosalyn Terborg Penn (Indiana University Press, 1993) 601.

[146] Linda M. Perkins, "Institute for Colored Youth, Philadelphia", 601.

[147] Linda M. Perkins, "Institute for Colored Youth, Philadelphia", 601.

[148] Linda M. Perkins "Fanny Jackson Coppin" in *Black Women in America* eds. Darlene Clark Hine, Elsa Barkley Brown and Rosalyn Terborg Penn (Indiana University Press, 1993 283.

[149] Linda M. Perkins "Fanny Jackson Coppin," 283.

[150] Linda M. Perkins "Fanny Jackson Coppin," 283.

[151] Linda M. Perkins "Fanny Jackson Coppin," 282.

[152] Linda M. Perkins "Fanny Jackson Coppin," 283.

[153] Fanny Jackson Coppin, *Reminiscences* 122.

[154] Fanny Jackson Coppin, *Reminiscences* 48.

[155] Hallie Quinn Brown, *Homespun Heroines and Other Women of Distinction* (New York: Oxford University Press, 1988), 74.

[156] Deborah Gray White *Ar'n't I A Woman?: Female Slaves in the Plantation South* (New York: W.W. Norton & Co., 1999), 170.

[157] Hallie Quinn Brown, *Homespun Heroines*, 71.

[158] Hallie Quinn Brown, *Homespun Heroines*, 74.

[159] The Underground Railroad was a secret, vast network of people, places, and modes of transportation that assisted fugitive enslaved people to gain their freedom. Chased by brutal 'slave catchers,' African Americans fleeing the Slaveocracy "…waded through swamps, concealed themselves in the hulls of ships, hid on the backs of carriages, and navigated circuitous routes by using the North Star at night—always with the understanding that they might be caught or betrayed at any time." Vigilance Committees, formed and manned by free African Americans like Thomas and Frances Brown, in cities such as Boston and Philadelphia, provided fugitive slaves with food, clothing, and shelter at great personal risk to themselves.

Source: Alonford James Robinson, "Underground Railroad," Microsoft ® Encarta ® Africana. © & (p) 1999 Microsoft Corporation.

[160] Hallie Quinn Brown, *Homespun Heroines*, 74.

[161] Hallie Quinn Brown, *Homespun Heroines*, 74.

[162] Hallie Quinn Brown, *Homespun Heroines*, 72.

[163] Hallie Quinn Brown, *Homespun Heroines*, 75.

[164] Hallie Quinn Brown, *Homespun Heroines*, 75.

[165] Hallie Quinn Brown, *Homespun Heroines*, 75.

[166] Hallie Quinn Brown, *Homespun Heroines*, 74.

[167] Hallie Quinn Brown, *Homespun Heroines*, 75.

[168] Hallie Quinn Brown, *Homespun Heroines*, 77.

[169] Hallie Quinn Brown, *Homespun Heroines*, 78.

[170] Hallie Quinn Brown, *Homespun Heroines*, 79.

[171] Hallie Quinn Brown, *Homespun Heroines*, 78.

[172] Vivian Njeri Fisher "Hallie Quinn Brown" in *Black Women in America* eds Darlene Clark Hine, Elsa Barkley Brown and Rosalyn Terborg-Penn (Indiana University Press, 1993) 177.

[173] Fannie Barrier Williams, "A Northern Negro's Autobiography" in *Black Defiance*; ed. Jay David (New York: William Morrow & Co., 1972) 73.

[174] Fannie Barrier Williams, "A Northern Negro's Autobiography," 74.

[175] Fannie Barrier Williams, "A Northern Negro's Autobiography," 76.

[176] Fannie Barrier Williams, "A Northern Negro's Autobiography," 75.

[177] Fannie Barrier Williams, "A Northern Negro's Autobiography," 75.

[178] Fannie Barrier Williams, "A Northern Negro's Autobiography," 76.

[179] Fannie Barrier Williams, "A Northern Negro's Autobiography," 76.

[180] Fannie Barrier Williams, "A Northern Negro's Autobiography," 76.

[181] Fannie Barrier Williams, "A Northern Negro's Autobiography," 77.

[182] Fannie Barrier Williams, "A Northern Negro's Autobiography" 80.

[183] Fannie Barrier Williams, "A Northern Negro's Autobiography" 81.

[184] Fannie Barrier Williams, "A Northern Negro's Autobiography," 81.

[185] Wanda Hendricks "Fannie Barrier Williams" in *Black Women in America* 843.

[186] Fannie Barrier Williams *A New Negro for a New Century* (New York: The Arno Press, 1969) 383.

[187] Leona C. Gabel, *From Slavery to the Sorbonne and Beyond: The Life and Writings of Anna J. Cooper* (North Hampton, Massachusetts: Department of History of Smith College, 1982) 12.

[188] Leona C. Gabel, *From Slavery to the Sorbonne and Beyond* 14.

[189] Anna Julia Cooper "The Higher Education of Women" in *The Voice of Anna Julia Cooper* eds. Charles Lemert and Esme Bhan (Lanham, Maryland: Rowman & Littlefield Publishers, 1998) 86.

[190] Leona C. Gabel, *From Slavery to the Sorbonne and Beyond: The Life and Writings of Anna J. Cooper* (North Hampton, Massachusetts: Department of History of Smith College, 1982) 17.

[191] Leona C. Gabel, *From Slavery to the Sorbonne and Beyond* 25.

[192] Leona C. Gabel, *From Slavery to the Sorbonne and Beyond* 61.

[193] Leona C. Gabel, *From Slavery to the Sorbonne and Beyond* 62.

[194] Leona C. Gabel, *From Slavery to the Sorbonne and Beyond* 69.

[195] Alfreda M. Duster ed. *Crusade for Justice: The Autobiography of Ida B. Wells* (University of Chicago Press, 1970) 9.

[195] Ida B. Wells, *Crusade for Justice*, 17.

[196] Ida B. Wells, *Crusade for Justice*, 19.

[197] Ida B. Wells, *Crusade for Justice*, 22.

[199] Ida B. Wells, *Crusade for Justice*, 23.

[200] Ida B. Wells, *Crusade for Justice*, 24.

[201] Ida B. Wells, *Crusade for Justice*, 42.

[202] Ida B. Wells, *Crusade for Justice*, 47.

[203] Ida B. Wells, *Crusade for Justice*, 64.

[204] Ida B. Wells, *Crusade for Justice*, 64.

[205] Ida B. Wells, *Crusade for Justice*, 70.

[206] Ida B. Wells, *Crusade for Justice*, 66.

[207] Ida B. Wells, *Crusade for Justice*, 62.

[208] Ida B. Wells, *Crusade for Justice*, 69.

[209] Ida B. Wells, *Crusade for Justice*, 78.

[210] Ida B. Wells, *Crusade for Justice*, 81.

[211] Ida B. Wells, *Crusade for Justice*, 82.

[212] Wanda Hendricks "Ida Bell Wells-Barnett" in *Black Women in America* 1242.

[213] Wanda Hendricks "Ida Bell Wells-Barnett" in *Black Women in America* 1242.

[214] Ida B. Wells, *Crusade for Justice*, 345.

[215] Evelyn Brooks Higginbotham, "African American Women's History and the Metalanguage of Race," in *We Specialize in the Wholly Impossible* eds., Darlene Clark Hine, Wilma King and Linda Reed (New York: Carlson Publishing, 1995) 1.

[216] Linda Gordon "Black and White Visions of Welfare,"158.

[217] Sarah Jane Early "The Great Part Taken by the Women of the West in the Development of the African Methodist Episcopal Church" in *The Three Sarahs* eds. Ellen NicKenzie Lawson and Marlene D. Merril, 175.

[218] Fanny Jackson Coppin *Reminiscences of School Life, and Hints on Teaching,* 117.

[219] Fanny Jackson Coppin *Reminiscences of School Life, and Hints on Teaching,* 119.

[220] Charles Lemert and Esme Bhan ed. *The Voice of Anna Julia Cooper,* 41.

[221] Charles Lemert and Esme Bhan ed. *The Voice of Anna Julia Cooper,* 41.

[222] Charles Lemert and Esme Bhan ed. *The Voice of Anna Julia Cooper,* 19.

[223] Charles Lemert and Esme Bhan ed. *The Voice of Anna Julia Cooper,* 3.

[224] Charles Lemert and Esme Bhan ed. *The Voice of Anna Julia Cooper*, 19.

[225] Charles Lemert and Esme Bhan ed. *The Voice of Anna Julia Cooper*, 19.

[226] Charles Lemert and Esme Bhan ed. *The Voice of Anna Julia Cooper*, 59.

[227] Leona C. Gabel, *From Slavery to the Sorbonne and Beyond*, 11.

[228] Leona C. Gabel, *From Slavery to the Sorbonne and Beyond*, 7.

[229] Leona C. Gabel, *From Slavery to the Sorbonne and Beyond*, 60.

[230] Anna Julia Cooper "The Higher Education of Women" in *The Voice of Anna Julia Cooper*, 76.

[231] Leona C. Gabel, *From Slavery to the Sorbonne and Beyond*, 85.

[232] Leona C. Gabel, *From Slavery to the Sorbonne and Beyond*, 50.

[233] Leona C. Gabel, *From Slavery to the Sorbonne and Beyond*, 87.

[234] Anna Julia Cooper "Womanhood: A Vital Element in the Regeneration and Progress of a Race" in *The Voice of Anna Julia Cooper*, 63.

[235] Ida B. Wells *Crusade for Justice*, 62.

[236] Ida B. Wells *Crusade for Justice*, 69.

[237] Ida B. Wells *Crusade for Justice*, 70.

[238] Barbara Welter "The Cult of True Womanhood" in *American Quarterly* 18 (1966) 158.

[239] Barbara Welter "The Cult of True Womanhood, 155.

[240] Barbara Welter "The Cult of True Womanhood, 159.

[241] Ida B. Wells *On Lynchings: Southern Horrors, A Red Record and Mob Rule in New Orleans* (New York: The Arno Press, 1969) 11.

[242] Ida B. Wells *Crusade for Justice*, 71; my emphasis.

[243] Ida B. Wells "Southern Horrors," 14.

[244] Ida B. Wells "Southern Horrors, 14.

[245] Ida B. Wells "Southern Horrors," 21.

[246] Ida B. Wells "Southern Horrors," 23.

[247] Ida B. Wells "Southern Horrors," 23.

[248] Ida B. Wells *Crusade for Justice*, 70.

[249] Ida B. Wells "Southern Horrors," 23.

[250] Gail Bederman *Manliness and Civilization: A Cultural History of Gender and Race in the United States, 1880–1917* (The University of Chicago Press, 1995) 23.

[251] Gail Bederman *Manliness and Civilization*, 10.

[252] Gail Bederman *Manliness and Civilization*, 45.

[253] Gail Bederman *Manliness and Civilization*, 49.

[254] Gail Bederman *Manliness and Civilization*, 48.

[255] Ida B. Wells, *Crusade for Justice*, 69.

[256] Ida B. Wells, *On Lynching*, 20.

[257] Ida B. Wells, *On Lynching*, 22.

[258] Hallie Quinn Brown, *Homespun Heroines*, 27.

[259] Hallie Quinn Brown, *Homespun Heroines*, 47.

[260] Hallie Quinn Brown, *Homespun Heroines*, 55.

[261] Hallie Quinn Brown, *Homespun Heroines*, 57.

[262] Hallie Quinn Brown, *Homespun Heroines*, 104.

[263] Hallie Quinn Brown, *Homespun Heroines*, 105.

[264] Hallie Quinn Brown, *Homespun Heroines*, 106.

[265] Hallie Quinn Brown, *Homespun Heroines*, 106.

[266] Hallie Quinn Brown, *Homespun Heroines*, 106.

[267] Darlene Clark Hine *Hine Sight: Black Women and the Re-Construction of American History* (Brooklyn, New York: Carlson Publishing, 1994) xxii.

[268] Hallie Quinn Brown, *Homespun Heroines*, vii.

[269] Hallie Quinn Brown, *Homespun Heroines*, vii.

[270] Darlene Clark Hine, *Hine Sight*, xxii.

[271] Darlene Clark Hine, *Hine Sight*, xxiii.

[272] Frances Ellen Watkins Harper "I Have a Right to Do My Share" (Tiffin, Ohio March 31, 1859) in *A Brighter Coming Day* Frances Smith Foster ed. (New York: The Feminist Press, 1990) 47.

[273] Frances Smith Foster, *A Brighter Coming Day*, 3.

[274] Frances Smith Foster, *A Brighter Coming Day*, 8.

[275] Frances Smith Foster, *A Brighter Coming Day*, 8.

[276] Frances Smith Foster, *A Brighter Coming Day*, 10.

[277] Frances Smith Foster, *A Brighter Coming Day*, 10.

[278] Frances Smith Foster, *A Brighter Coming Day*, 10.

[279] Frances Smith Foster, *A Brighter Coming Day*, 11.

[280] Frances Smith Foster, *A Brighter Coming Day*, 12.

[281] Frances Smith Foster, *A Brighter Coming Day*, 12.

[282] Frances Smith Foster, *A Brighter Coming Day*, 12.

[283] Frances Ellen Watkins Harper "The Colored People of America" in *A Brighter Coming Day* ed Frances Smith Foster (New York: The Feminist Press, 1990) 100.

[284] Frances Ellen Watkins Harper "The Agent of the State Anti-Slavery Society of Maine Travels with Me," 44.

[285] Frances Smith Foster, *A Brighter Coming Day*, 15.

[286] Frances Smith Foster, *A Brighter Coming Day*, 15.

[287] Frances Harper, "On Free Produce," *A Brighter Coming Day*, 45.

[288] Frances Harper, *A Brighter Coming Day*, 16.

[289] Frances Harper, *A Brighter Coming Day*, 16.

[290] Frances Harper, "Oh How I Miss England," *A Brighter Coming Day*, 47.

[291] Frances Harper, "On Free Produce," *A Brighter Coming Day*, 45.

[292] Frances Harper, "My Lungs Are Weak...I Need Rest," *A Brighter Coming Day*, 50.

[293] Frances Harper, "My Lungs Are Weak...I Need Rest," *A Brighter Coming Day*, 50.

[294] Frances Harper, "I Am Able to Give Something," *A Brighter Coming Day*, 52.

[295] Fannie Barrier Williams, "Do We Need Another Name?" *The New Woman of Color*, 84.

[296] Fannie Barrier Williams, "Do We Need Another Name?" *The New Woman of Color*, 85.

[297] Charles Lemert and Esme Bhan ed. *The Voice of Anna Julia Cooper*, 50.

[298] Charles Lemert and Esme Bhan ed. *The Voice of Anna Julia Cooper*, 50.

[299] Fannie Barrier Williams, "The Problem of Employment for Negro Women," *The New Woman of Color*, 56.

[300] Fannie Barrier Williams, "The Problem of Employment for Negro Women," *The New Woman of Color*, 52.

[301] Fannie Barrier Williams, "The Problem of Employment for Negro Women," *The New Woman of Color*, 54.

[302] Fannie Barrier Williams, "The Problem of Employment for Negro Women," *The New Woman of Color*, 55.

[303] Fannie Barrier Williams, "The Problem of Employment for Negro Women," *The New Woman of Color*, 56.

[304] Fannie Barrier Williams, "The Problem of Employment for Negro Women," *The New Woman of Color*, 55.

[305] Fannie Barrier Williams, "The Problem of Employment for Negro Women," *The New Woman of Color*, 55.

[306] Fannie Barrier Williams, "The Problem of Employment for Negro Women," *The New Woman of Color*, 53.

[307] Fannie Barrier Williams, "The Problem of Employment for Negro Women," *The New Woman of Color*, 55.

[308] Linda Gordon "Black and White Visions of Welfare: Women's Welfare Activism, 1890–1945" in *Unequal Sisters* eds. Vicki L. Ruiz and Ellen Carol DuBois, 163.

[309] Evelyn Brooks Higginbotham, *Righteous Discontent*, 42.

CHAPTER FOUR

[310] Benjamin C. Truman *History of the World's Fair* (Philadelphia: Mammoth Publishing Company, 1893) 120.

[2] Christopher Reed *All The World Is Here!*, 22.

[312] Benjamin C. Truman *History of the World's Fair* (Philadelphia: Mammoth Publishing Company, 1893) 120.

[313] F.L. Barnett, "The Reason Why," 6.

[314] F.L. Barnett, "The Reason Why," 6.

[315] F.L. Barnett, "The Reason Why," 6.

[316] Ann Massa "Black Women in the 'White City'" in *American Studies* 1969 8, 3, 320.

[317] Ann Massa "Black Women in the 'White City'," 323.

[318] Christopher Robert Reed *All The World Is Here!: The Black Presence at White City* (Indiana University Press, 2000) 22.

[319] F.L. Barnett "The Reason Why" in *The Reason Why*...9

[320] Ann Massa "Black Women in the 'White City'," 326.

[321] Ida B. Wells, "Miss Ida B. Wells Informs Our Readers as to the Condition of the World's Fair Pamphlet Movement," *Cleveland Gazette*, July 22, 1893, p. 1.

[322] Ida B. Wells, *Crusade for Justice: The Autobiography of Ida B. Wells* ed. Alfreda M. Duster (The University of Chicago Press, 1970) 117.

[323] Ida B. Wells, "Preface" 2.

[324] Frederick Douglass, "Chapter One: Introduction," 12.

[325] Frederick Douglass, "Chapter One: Introduction," 13.

[326] I. Garland Penn, "The Progress of the Afro-American Since Emancipation" in *The Reason Why the Colored American Is Not at The World's Columbian Exposition* ed. Ida B. Wells in *Women and Social Movements, 1775–2000* © 1997–2003 by Thomas Dublin and Kathryn Kish Sklar, 6.

[327] Christopher Robert Reed *All the World Is Here!: The Black Presence at White City* (Bloomington, Indiana: Indiana University Press, 2000) xiii.

[328] Ida B. Wells, *A Crusade for* Justice, 116.

[329] Christopher Robert Reed, *All the World Is Here!*, xiii.

[330] Christopher Robert Reed, *All the World Is Here!*, x.

[331] Christopher Robert Reed, *All the World Is Here!*, x.

[332] Ann Massa "Black Women in the 'White City'," 331.

[333] Hallie Quinn Brown "The World's Fair" *The Cleveland Gazette* April 16, 1892.

[334] F.L. Barnett "The Reason Why" in *The Reason Why*...11.

[335] Ann Massa "Black Women in the 'White City'," 332.

[336] Ann Massa "Black Women in the 'White City'," 333.

[337] Ann Massa "Black Women in the 'White City'," 333.

[338] May Wright Sewell. *The World's Congress of Representative Women: The World's Congress Auxiliary* (Chicago: Rand, McNally and Co., 1894) 2.

[339] May Wright Sewell. *The World's Congress of Representative Women*, 4.

[340] May Wright Sewell. *The World's Congress of Representative Women*, 4.

[341] Jeanne Weimann. *The Fair Women* (Chicago Academy, 1981) 524.

[342] May Wright Sewall, *The World's Congress of Representative Women*, 6.

[343] May Wright Sewall, *The World's Congress of Representative Women*, 929.

[344] May Wright Sewall, *The World's Congress of Representative Women*, 16

[345] May Wright Sewall. *The World's Congress of Representative Women*, 7.

[346] May Wright Sewall. *The World's Congress of Representative Women*, xxii.

[347] Fanny Jackson Coppin, "The Intellectual Progress of the Colored Women of the United States Since the Emancipation Proclamation," 716.

[348] Frances Ellen Watkins Harper "Woman's Political Future" in *The World's Congress of Representative Women: The World's Congress Auxiliary* ed. May Wright Sewell (Chicago: Rand, McNally and Co., 1894) 433.

[349] Frances Ellen Watkins Harper "Woman's Political Future," 434.

[350] Frances Ellen Watkins Harper "Woman's Political Future," 435.

[351] Frances Ellen Watkins Harper "Woman's Political Future," 435.

[352] Frances Ellen Watkins Harper "Woman's Political Future," 436.

[353] Fannie Barrier Williams, "The Intellectual Progress of the Colored Women of the United States," 697.

[354] Fannie Barrier Williams, "The Intellectual Progress of the Colored Women of the United States," 702.

[355] Fannie Barrier Williams, "The Intellectual Progress of the Colored Women of the United States," 703.

[356] Fannie Barrier Williams, "The Intellectual Progress of the Colored Women of the United States," 704.

[357] Fannie Barrier Williams, "The Intellectual Progress of the Colored Women of the United States Since the Emancipation Proclamation," 699.

[358] Fannie Barrier Williams, "The Intellectual Progress of the Colored Women of the United States Since the Emancipation Proclamation," 705.

[359] Fannie Barrier Williams, "The Intellectual Progress of the Colored Women of the United States Since the Emancipation Proclamation," 706.

[360] Fannie Barrier Williams, "The Intellectual Progress of the Colored Women of the United States Since the Emancipation Proclamation," 710.

[361] Fannie Barrier Williams, "The Intellectual Progress of the Colored Women of the United States Since the Emancipation Proclamation," 710.

[362] Anna Julia Cooper, "The Intellectual Progress of the Colored Women of the United States Since the Emancipation Proclamation in *The World's Congress of Representative Women* ed. May Wright Sewall (Chicago: Rand, McNally & Co., 1894) 711.

[363] Anna Julia Cooper, "The Intellectual Progress of the Colored Women of the United States Since the Emancipation Proclamation," 711.

[364] Anna Julia Cooper, "The Intellectual Progress of the Colored Women of the United States Since the Emancipation Proclamation," 712.

[365] Anna Julia Cooper, "The Intellectual Progress of the Colored Women of the United States Since the Emancipation Proclamation," 713.

[366] Anna Julia Cooper, "The Intellectual Progress of the Colored Women of the United States Since the Emancipation Proclamation," 714.

[367] Fanny Jackson Coppin, "The Intellectual Progress of the Colored Women of the United States Since the Emancipation Proclamation," 716.

[368] Fanny Jackson Coppin, "The Intellectual Progress of the Colored Women of the United States Since the Emancipation Proclamation," 716.

[369] Sarah Jane Early, "The Organized Efforts of the Colored Women Of the South to Improve Their Condition," 718.

[370] Sarah Jane Early, "The Organized Efforts of the Colored Women Of the South to Improve Their Condition," 718.

[371] Sarah Jane Early, "The Organized Efforts of the Colored Women Of the South to Improve Their Condition," 719.

[372] Sarah Jane Early, "The Organized Efforts of the Colored Women Of the South to Improve Their Condition," 720.

[373] Sarah Jane Early, "The Organized Efforts of the Colored Women Of the South to Improve Their Condition," 723.

[374] Sarah Jane Early, "The Organized Efforts of the Colored Women Of the South to Improve Their Condition," 724.

[375] Hallie Quinn Brown, "The Organized Efforts of the Colored Women Of the South to Improve Their Condition," 724.

[376] Hallie Quinn Brown, "The Organized Efforts of the Colored Women Of the South to Improve Their Condition," 724.

[377] Hallie Quinn Brown, "The Intellectual Progress of the Colored Women of the United States Since the Emancipation Proclamation", 725.

[378] Hallie Quinn Brown, "The Intellectual Progress of the Colored Women of the United States Since the Emancipation Proclamation", 727.

[379] Hallie Quinn Brown, "The Intellectual Progress of the Colored Women of the United States Since the Emancipation Proclamation", 727.

[380] Hallie Quinn Brown, "The Organized Efforts of the Colored Women Of the South to Improve Their Condition," 729.

[381] Gail Bederman, *Manliness & Civilization: A Cultural History of Gender and Race in the United States, 1880–1917* (Chicago: The University of Chicago Press, 1995) 10.

[382] Hazel V. Carby *Reconstructing Womanhood* (New York: Oxford University Press, 1987) 30.

[383] Hazel V. Carby *Reconstructing Womanhood*, 32.

[384] Hazel V. Carby *Reconstructing Womanhood*, 97.

978-0-595-40687-6
0-595-40687-4

CPSIA information can be obtained
at www.ICGtesting.com
Printed in the USA
LVHW031752260121
677549LV00005B/944